The Art of WEATHERING

BY
MARTYN WELCH

WILD SWAN PUBLICATIONS

ISBN 1 874103 11 9

FOR HELEN

Designed by Paul Karau
Printed by The Amadeus Press,
Cleckheaton, West Yorkshire.

Published by
WILD SWAN PUBLICATIONS LTD.
1 - 3 Hagbourne Road, Didcot, Oxon OX11 8DP

INTRODUCTION

A 7mm scale Malcolm Mitchell '44XX' sitting atop the embankment in late afternoon sun.

WHETHER TO WEATHER

For as long as I can remember there has been heated debate concerning the way a model railway should look. Part of the problem is that the hobby cannot be easily defined or categorised because there are so many different reasons why we start modelling in the first place. Similarly, the end results required are rarely the same for each of us.

When layouts are featured in magazines, most of us are not so daft that we don't realise we're looking at models but a clever photograph of a well weathered item can sometimes give rise to serious eyebrow twitching. But if done badly, it can look pretty grim and if poor examples are all that you have ever seen in the modelling press or at exhibitions, then that would quite understandably have made you hesitate before taking the plunge or even have put you off the idea completely.

Now I have been assaulting models since I was knee high to a ferret, attempting to make my creations look just that little bit more representative of the railways seen all around me. I believe creating a model which could easily be taken for reality when seen in an authentic setting to be an art form in itself and far from 'ruining' a model, feel the reverse is the case.

I certainly don't consider myself expert at it – I have simply spent many years experimenting with different procedures so that a certain amount of knowledge or experience has been built up into a set of routines which I find work for me. Trial by combat, so to speak. I have found that what might appear to be a complicated process is in fact just a logical sequence of events and most of the procedures take longer to explain than to actually perform.

If your hobby simply involves collecting together an assortment of railway items, each of which is in its original production finish, then you probably won't want to consider weathering anything in the first place. On the other hand, if you prefer to see a realistic impression of those same items and their environment, it means that everything will require weathering to some degree in order that the entire effect should appear natural. Look out of your window and see if you can spot anything which doesn't show the slightest evidence of weathering by the elements or the human touch – I very much doubt you will.

Of course there are many who feel the whole idea of inflicting dirt and grime upon their glorious creations is a mortal sin and that railways should only appear as spotlessly clean wonders of transport delight. For

those who cannot accept the thought of tarnishing that golden image which has been created solely in their own minds, then fair enough – life's too short to make an issue of it.

Reality shows the railways to have been rather dirty, unhealthy and seldom able to live up to their publicity department's optimistic claims. However, the keen enthusiast who came home at the end of a day's train-spotting covered in soot and grime, but usually bearing a look of happy contentment, didn't worry about such things, and if you fall into this category or can relate to that image, then perhaps you are already attempting to model things as they really are and what follows may therefore be of interest to you.

I much prefer to view the processes which we shall experience in the ensuing pages as logical ways of adding 'Realism' to our models – to take the straightforward squeaky clean locomotive, wagon, etc, from the realms of toyland into an entirely more satisfying area of modelling skills. For the sake of simplicity, though, I shall carry on using the term 'weathering' since that is the word which has become familiar to most.

Many years ago, I attended an exhibition where I saw a really fine example of weath-

First impressions are of a very neat loco with burnished handrails, dart and door hinges. The cleaners have been busy but the smokebox and chimney paint is scorched and peeling.
L & GRP, CTY. DAVID & CHARLES

ering which had been carried out on an American outline locomotive. It was extremely convincing and I asked the chap seated behind the stand if he would perhaps explain how he had gone about it, to which he replied: 'If I told everybody who asked me, they'd all be able to do it, wouldn't they?' Feeling rather perplexed by his somewhat frosty response and casting caution to the wind, I enquired as to whether that would be such a bad thing and even had the temerity to suggest that passing his knowledge on to others might be very rewarding to all parties concerned – his withering glare said it all.

With his words echoing in my mind, maybe the following will not only answer questions concerning how I've weathered my models but, in so doing, perhaps encourage others to have a go for themselves.

RESEARCH

Assuming you have decided to work on the appearance of your models to make them look more convincingly like the full-size originals, you are no doubt wondering where to start. You may wish first of all to work out why the real thing looks as it does and with steam locomotives, for example, the very fact that they throw out soot, ash, oil and water in varying quantities and directions and are then subjected to the ravages of Mother Nature in scorching sun, pouring rain, snow, ice, etc, the end result is not surprisingly a fairly complex array of stains, streaks, patches of rust and so on. General wear and tear will cause paint to peel, dents, scuffs, scratches and smears from the human touch will add to the total visual effect, and the end result is a real hotch-potch of varying textures and colours. Observation is your main ally and if you fastidiously copy the blemishes, stains and other effects as you see them on the full-size item, you should end up with a convincing miniature replica.

As a start then, I suggest you spend some time sorting through photographs in magazines and books, studying them in close detail. Ideally these photographs should be in colour since that is how you are going to learn to recognise the subtle tones which most frequently appear as rust stains or patches of oil, or just simply coatings of soot and general traffic grime. Having said that, even black and white photographs will show up the various shades and highlights, often giving clearer definition to the finer detail.

Every item of stock is different and each will react to weathering and maltreatment in varying ways. As you wander from photo to photo, you will start to notice a number of common patterns in the way, for example, that certain colour paints fade more drastically than others and how unpainted timber on wagons has a grey/beige tint rather than the light brown most seem to imagine wood to be. Rust stains have a tendency to streak vertically rather than horizontally and add subtle colour changes to the affected timber and so on.

If you have a camera of your own, you can visit preserved lines or, if your appetite is for more modern stock, your local loco depot or station will enable you to study your chosen favourite and take your own photographs of the relevant items. On many occasions I have received puzzled looks from passengers at my local station because the average spotter with a camera is usually taking general shots of approaching trains whereas I am invariably to be found stooped down with the lens pointing somewhat precariously at a really interesting patch of rust on the underframe of a lone wagon parked at the end of the platform.

It seems there will always be vigorous debate concerning what colour an item may have originally been and what shade it changed to after a few months' service etc, but I shan't travel that route for the sake of peace and a quiet life. It's much more important that the colour you finally

This one photograph is crammed full of detail with just about every conceivable sign of wear and tear begging to be modelled.   P. SIMPSON

choose should look right to you as you see it or remember seeing it, rather than how someone else claims it to appear – besides, there are many reasons why we each see certain colours as we do – some of which are quite straightforward and others leave me twiddling my thumbs and wishing I hadn't asked in the first place. Whilst it is sometimes useful to know these things, creating these effects mercifully doesn't require that knowledge in great detail. In most cases, it is only a matter of thinking logically about how that effect may have been created in reality, then discovering some way of either copying the process artificially, or giving the illusion that such processes have taken place.

Now we're getting to the nub of the matter as I see it. Illusion. As I hinted in the introduction, we're most of us rowing the river of life with all our oars in the water (although there are some days when I do wonder . . .) and common sense tells us we're unlikely to ever achieve total reality with our models, but with a little thought we can at least get pretty close to a convincing *illusion* of reality.

Perhaps some simple thoughts on colour may be of assistance, at this stage and we'll take black as an example because, in the strictest sense, black isn't defined as a colour in itself but the end result of combining all other colours of the spectrum. (Did I say 'simple thoughts'?) Remove any one of the colours and you have a subtle shade change, but if you then imagine removing or adding just small percentages of each colour to one or any group of the remaining colours then the mind really starts to wobble a bit as the possibilities present themselves. Ask any professional car sprayer the most difficult colour to match and I'll lay odds the answer will be 'black'.

It is possible to work out some of the colours' constituent parts for yourself. If you find a picture in a railway book or magazine which you feel really captures the colour of your favourite locomotive or whatever else you fancy duplicating, take a powerful magnifying glass and you will see the printed picture is made up of lots of tiny dots or speckles. The printer has to analyse the colour content of the original transparency and this will then be translated into certain percentages of basic colours to duplicate the original photograph – but in the dot form you see under the glass. If he has done his work properly, you can be fairly certain that this is an accurate rendition of the original. Now the tricky part is to be able to work out for yourself what

proportions of red, yellow, blue and probably black dots have been printed in relation to the white background colour of the paper. If you can calculate this and then mix your paints accordingly, you should be able to reproduce that same colour for yourself. If the end result looks the same as the picture in the book, you've done it!

You may be thinking that if everything's going to be as complicated as all that, you may not wish to read further – but I assure you this will not be the case. That was just an example of one particular method of analysing colour composition taught to me when I served my apprenticeship as a lithographic artist in the printing trade. It isn't easy, I will agree, but it saves a heck of a lot of argument if you can master it.

What will probably surprise you is the make-up of that favourite colour. Green is usually accepted as being a mixture of yellow and blue, but look closely at Brunswick Green under the eye glass in the printed picture and see how much red is in there as well.

If you really cannot be fussed to go to such lengths – and I'm not suggesting you need to – then just try matching your paints to the colours you see in your photographs and if you're happy that it's close enough, then away you go. However, if you're wondering what colour rust really is and you wish to copy that colour precisely, then at

least the eye glass will show you in the printed picture just what the constituent colours are which make up that particular shade of rust. I have yet to find any rust which is even close to being a simple brick red and yet the little tins of paint sold in model shops have 'rust' printed on the lid and are usually just a lighter or darker version of that red. Most modellers happily paint their models with it without questioning the accuracy of the manufacturer's chosen shade. Some of the more specialist paint suppliers are starting to recognise that this is not the way it should be and at least are trying to offer general ranges of 'weathered' colours which offer better options. I find the varieties of colour and textures which result from rusted metal to be quite fascinating and in certain lights have a beauty all their own. Yes, well perhaps I am a little more peculiar than most!

When I studied art at school, the art master gave me one sound piece of advice which I should like to pass on to you: 'Paint what you see, not what you *think* you see – then if it looks right, it probably is.'

Observation, then is probably the keyword at this stage and if you're still with me and haven't decided counting blades of grass would probably be much more interesting, then I'll meander into the next section.

Hursley was my first attempt at layout construction and in this cameo scene, the station master seems to pose for the camera as an 'M7' pauses between duties in bright sunshine.

MATERIALS AND EQUIPMENT

PAINTS

Most paints are hazardous to health if inhaled and I must add a word of caution – ALWAYS apply spray paint in a well ventilated area and even if you're simply hand brushing using enamels and thinners, do ensure that the room you're working in has a window open. For spray work, I ALWAYS wear a face mask and use an area in the garage near to the open up-and-over door which ensures a clean draught of air at all times. If it's too cold or damp to leave the door open, go and sit by the fire with a favourite book for this is not the day to be spraying anyway. Don't shut yourself in a confined airless place with a heater on – you may not live to regret it.

Cellulose

There are many high quality enamel paints on the market which will provide an excellent finish if applied carefully, but I use cellulose if possible for the main body colour of locomotives and coaches (the term 'main body colour' signifies the ex-works paint finish prior to any weathering). I say 'if possible', because cellulose can easily be applied to metal-based models but can be fairly destructive to plastics unless applied in very fine coats which dry almost instantly before any damage can be done and an airbrush is vital to achieve a smooth finish in small quantities at a time.

Cellulose has a very rapid drying time which virtually eliminates the risk of dust settling on the paint and becoming irretrievably embedded in it. Because it does dry so quickly, it is very tricky to apply by brush so unless you do have an airbrush to hand, you would be wise to forget cellulose as your chosen medium unless you are really skilled with the car aerosol cans of paint found in most car accessory shops. These are naturally designed to spray cars rather than our models and tend to plonk a fairly dense coat over large areas at a time. Apart from its rapid drying time, I favour cellulose for the following reasons:

1. The end result is a smooth and exceptionally hard paint finish which can be handled quite freely without fear of leaving fingerprints or smudges.
2. It accepts lining and transfers readily and, of particular significance for us, if you weather it using enamels and then want to remove some of the weathering either for effect, or because you've made

a complete pig's ear of it, you can use enamel thinners to dissolve the paint without any risk of removing the main body colour. If the base colour is enamel paint, you do chance removing more than you bargained for which can be very frustrating.

In order to obtain the correct colours in cellulose, there is usually at least one motor trade paint supplier in your area who will be able to mix paints to your specification if you ask. Take along a sample of enamel paint or an item which is as near to the colour as possible and the supplier should be able to take it out to his workshop where the colour can be analysed and a pot of cellulose mixed to order. Failing that, he will certainly have several colour charts from which to select a perfect match for your chosen hue and he will then be able to mix it accordingly. These colour charts will also indicate that the paint may have a British Standards Number (B.S. for short) and this will in turn have a description of how that colour is made up in percentages of primary colours. You could therefore mix your own paints at home if you purchase some of the basic constituent colours such as red, yellow, blue, black and white.

Cellulose paint is not cheap and a small pot in car trade terms is enormous in ours. A litre tin will cost around £10 to £15 but will last you forever if kept well sealed in storage. Alternatively, the local Halfords or large DIY store usually keeps a com-

prehensive range of paints and many railway finishes are often easily recognisable although usually described by some exotic name to suit the car concerned. The final alternative is to get to know a local garage where painting work is carried out and ask to buy any old cans which they invariably have lying around in some dusty paint store. They frequently have more than they need for a particular customer's requirements and half full cans may be found lining their shelves, never to be needed again. The garage proprietor will probably not ask too much for the paint, if indeed he charges you at all. Cellulose thinners is available from DIY stores and car accessory shops.

Enamels

If you prefer to use enamels for the main body colours, a basic selection of railway liveries is available from several sources. Humbrol offer a limited range of colours, some of which are (in my opinion) a bit suspect in their authenticity, while Precision Paints have in the past been considered quite acceptable from the colour accuracy point of view but I have found their covering power somewhat questionable and their availability doubtful.

Railmatch paints are a more recent introduction using high quality coaching enamels as does the perhaps less well-known range from Cherry Scale Models. Each has enabled the modeller to choose almost any authentic finish of extremely

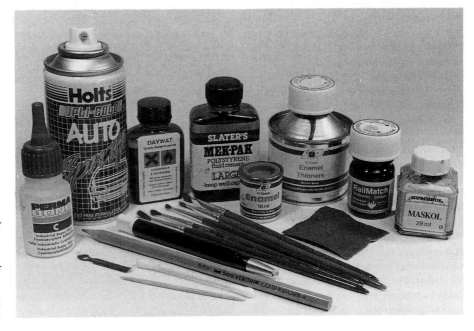

high quality. These coaching enamels which are much harder than the traditional enamels can be relied upon to give a smooth brush finish as well as being perfect for airbrushing.

When it comes to the actual weathering, I prefer to use matt enamels as sold in all good model shops. Humbrol have been around for a long time and most modellers are familiar with their paints, although in recent times I have found them rather prone to solidifying in the can and some of the 'matt' colours occasionally aren't. I now favour the paints made by Perkins (probably more familiar to you by their initials – JP on the cans) which are of a constantly high quality. This range utilises the same paint numbering as Humbrol so you don't need to learn a new coding system and the pigments are much finer and denser, requiring less coats to cover a given area. I have yet to discover a faulty tinlet and it can be used straight from the pot without hours of stirring. The exception to my rule is the Humbrol 'Metalcote' range which is exclusive to that firm. When the paint has dried, it can be polished by buffing with a mop or finger, producing a high gloss sheen which is very useful for certain special effects.

Acrylics

With the exception of varnish, I have little experience of acrylic paints and cannot comment upon their suitability or otherwise for either topcoat or weathering. I have experimented a little with them but have found them less easy to apply and then alter if necessary. The colours in their wet state also seem to vary quite a lot from the dried finish which can create problems when trying to match colours.

AIRBRUSHES

There are some who believe that airbrushes are an unnecessary evil which should be avoided at all costs, but to achieve a really smooth paint finish and for some of the weathering effects, there is no real substitute for a decent airbrush – take the plunge and buy one along with a compressor if you can run to it. An initially frightening thought because of the expense, but, if you are going to do a lot of this in the future, you must weigh up the pros and cons of such an outlay. You may not wish to spend out on a compressor, and perhaps instead adapt a car tyre or keep buying those cans of aerosol propellant which have a tendency to freeze and every now and then splatter water droplets through the airbrush

Typical spray pattern produced from cheap splatter gun. This was presented to me as an example of good weathering!

which can be most upsetting. Painting and weathering one 7 mm loco will probably use up two or three aerosol propellant cans at a fiver or more each and it doesn't take a genius to realise how quickly the costs will mount up. You can expect to pay (at the time of writing) around £100 for quality compressors from several manufacturers and these are available from most stockists.

If you are only adding realism to models which already have the desired ex-works finish, then there are many weathering effects which can be carried out without even looking at an airbrush, and we will discuss these processes as they crop up. I paced up and down muttering to myself for days before deciding whether or not to splash out on my airbrush many moons ago but I have never regretted the purchase simply because I have yet to see a hand-brushed paint finish which will even closely compare with an airbrushed one. As far as I can see, it is impossible to apply a faint, even, subtle haze of paint by any other method and for an overall coating of traffic dust, for example, this is the only logical way to duplicate the process. It is an absolute must for many of the tasks ahead.

Before taking the plunge, perhaps a short section on the use and maintenance of airbrushes wouldn't go amiss – if you're already experienced in their use, please bear with me as there are many who seem to find the airbrush as mystifying as nuclear fission.

The trouble possibly starts with the mistaken notion that the cheap old splatter gun found in many hobby shops is a typical airbrush and when a customer gleefully parts with his funds and expects on arriving home to reproduce fine quality airbrushed paint finishes using this latest purchase, it comes as no surprise to me that success is not the word that comes to mind. It should be made clear that the item in question will spray paint roughly in the direction to which it is pointed, but in my experience the ability to spray anything other than a general application of paint over an almost uncontrollable area is in some doubt.

This is not your fault, it's just a case of the wrong tool for the job concerned. For spraying scenery or other large areas, it's possibly adequate at best. However, we wish to apply very small amounts of paint to sometimes tiny areas at a time, and for this we need to seek out a quality airbrush. There are several types to choose from which may appear a little bewildering at first glance, but I have found the double-action type the most useful. This enables one to control the amount of air and the quantity of paint at the same time which is rather important – it is also the most expensive because of its fine precision control. Usually with each airbrush, there will be an accompanying booklet which will explain basic techniques and may have a small example of fine lines actually sprayed from your new purchase before leaving the factory. This will show just how delicate a finish can be achieved with practice.

As a matter of personal preference, I favour a gravity-fed airbrush, i.e. one whose paint cup is mounted on top of the tool which permits paint to be drawn down into the nozzle by gravity. Ideally, the paint should be pre-mixed and then decanted into the cup, although I must confess to poor airbrush practice and frequently mix the paints with their appropriate thinners in the cup itself. Not to be recommended as this is a pretty effective way of permitting clots of paint to clog in the airbrush nozzle.

I currently use the DeVilbiss Sprite which is a gravity top-fed instrument and can recommend it as a fine quality unit. The Sprite Major produces the same results but differs in that it has its paint cups mounted below the instrument so that paint is sucked up into the airbrush instead. Fine and medium nozzles and needles are available for each – the latter will produce a wider spray pattern and is better for spraying larger areas at one go. As an alternative, I would suggest the Badger 100 airbrush with a small or medium top cup which again is available with fine or medium head assemblies.

It would take several pages and better qualified advice than I can offer to go into great depth concerning the artistry of airbrushing and there are several books available written by those who use the airbrush for a living, but I can offer a few basic tips as a general guide.

Before starting anything, I have to repeat that it is absolutely VITAL to wear a protective mask. A suitable mask for protecting your lungs from enamel and cellulose paints will cost about £15–£20 – an investment which could save your life. Cheap dust masks or a handkerchief held over your nose and mouth simply will not do the job. I have one which bears a striking resemblance to a World War 2 gas mask, but no matter how absurd you look, it's nothing to how you look when dead . . .

As a general guide, the greater the air pressure, the finer the atomisation of paint particles. If you use less air pressure, the particles of paint will be that much larger and you will produce a much coarser spray. So, if you wish to produce a finely spattered paint effect rather than a delicate misted finish, don't press the trigger down so far (air pressure is controlled by depressing the trigger) and pull it back towards you a little further (this increases the paint flow). This obviously applies only to double-action airbrushes, and for the less expensive units, the air and paint flow are increased or decreased with a single action by depressing the trigger. If you have a compressor fitted with a pressure gauge and control knob, you can decrease or increase the air pressure from

that. If you don't have this facility, then a simple trick to reduce the air pressure is just to crimp the air hose by folding it gently which will restrict the air flow accordingly. If both hands aren't free, tread gently on the hosepipe with your wellies!

Mixing the paint and thinners to the right consistency is very important and for cellulose I would suggest 20% paint – 80% thinners is the strongest the solution should be because it is so quick drying that any increase in the paint content will nearly always result in the airbrush nozzle clogging within a matter of seconds. Cellulose is a coarse paint which adds to the problem. Enamels can be mixed in opposite proportions with the larger percentage being the paint. Mix the enamels too thin and you will get poor coverage and paint running everywhere. Experiment on something of no value until you find the mixture to suit.

If applying a basic coat of paint, take several light passes across the surface of the model. Don't blast it with air and paint or it will run in all directions and flood uncontrollably. Start spraying to one side of the model on a scrap of paper and when you're happy that the right amount of paint is being sprayed, then pass lightly left to right (or vice versa) across the surface and

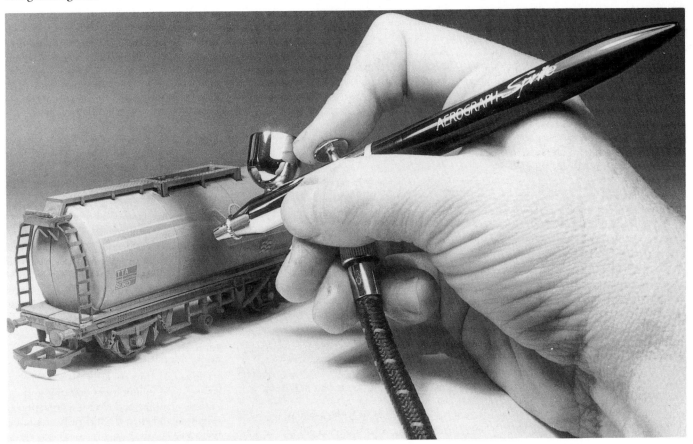

A quality airbrush permits really close work for the most delicate results.

don't stop spraying until you have passed beyond the model and onto another scrap of paper. For an even coat of paint, the intensity of colour should be identical on both pieces of paper. If you start or stop spraying whilst still aimed at the model, you run the risk of splatters or blobs of paint appearing as you release the trigger which might not be part of the required finish!

If you spray too close to the model using lots of air and paint, you will inevitably get runs and squiggles, so if you need to apply limited amounts to very small areas of a model which means getting the airbrush up close to avoid overspray, then go gently on the throttle. Let gentle puffs of air with tiny amounts of paint flow through the nozzle. Practise until you're sick to death of either the hobby or the smell of paint and thinners. Don't hurry the task. It's much better to build up thin layers of paint than to try getting a dense finish in one pass. If you're using enamels, you will have to permit each coat to become touch dry and this takes time. Cellulose dries quickly and the process is therefore faster, but even so, take your time.

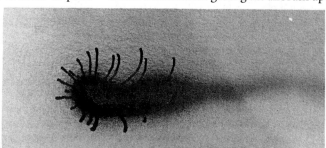

Too much paint flow at close range.

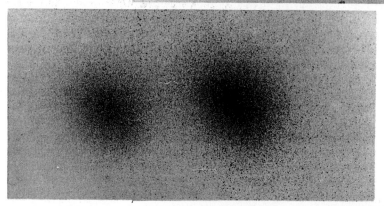

Not enough air pressure to atomise the paint.

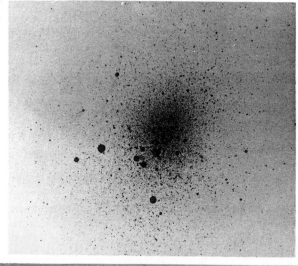

Starting the paint before the air (double action brush).

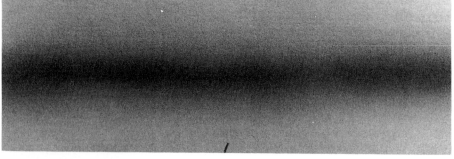

Start the air before the paint. O.K.

Many modellers comment that the airbrush clogs frequently or becomes totally blocked. Well it happens to all of us and for various reasons. Most commonly it is because the paint isn't thinned enough. The paint/air jet aperture in the nozzle of your airbrush can be measured in thousandths of an inch so if the paint is too thick, it simply will not pass through the hole without depositing some paint inside which builds up until the nozzle becomes blocked. The air passing through it starts to dry the paint, which will then partly solidify before it's had a chance to leave the airbrush nozzle.

The slightest impurity or foreign body entering the system will wreak havoc (which is why my habit of mixing paint in the airbrush cup is not very clever). Between changes of colour, clean the airbrush thoroughly – initially by spraying pure CELLULOSE thinners through the airbrush onto a scrap of paper or a light coloured cloth. It doesn't matter what paint you have been using, normal paint thinners or white spirit will not have the guts to dissolve any small clods of paint whereas cellulose thinners is very effective at dissolving enamels and most other types of paint.

When the thinners is no longer emerging with any tint of colour, it's safe to proceed with the next coat. If for any reason the airbrush does become clogged and you have one of the better airbrushes, you will be able to dismantle the mechanism with ease and clean the individual components such as the needle or nozzle. Small metal parts can be left to soak in jars of cellulose thinners for a few minutes to remove any stubborn build-up of paints, and finally lightly coat the needle with fine sewing machine oil before the airbrush is assembled again. At the end of every painting session, a full dismantling and cleaning operation is suggested and then the airbrush should be put away in its box for use next time. There's nothing more tedious than preparing to start spraying only to find that the airbrush is covered in paint from your last task and you then waste valuable time taking it apart and struggling to get the thing working again. You end up trying to remove lumps of paint using a sharp stick or worse, and this is not good airbrush practice.

Averaging about £100 per throw, the airbrush can be an expensive purchase and should be treated with respect. It is a precision instrument – don't abuse it.

WEATHERING POWDERS

Initially, I found the Carr's weathering powders and I didn't get along – I suspect my first impressions were not favourable because I had always used paints which stayed put once applied and found the powders rubbed off when the model was subsequently handled, so I therefore dismissed them as a waste of money and put my head back in the sand where it was safe and cosy.

However, at a recent exhibition, a colleague was exhibiting his 7 mm layout and I particularly admired a GWR pannier tootling past which was very nicely weathered and I asked which airbrush he'd used. To my astonishment, he said he hadn't used one but had used weathering powder instead. A loud clang was heard as my jaw dropped to the floor and I decided that perhaps I should take another look at Carr's products.

This time I thoroughly read the instructions or guide lines which accompany the powders (I had only skimped through them the first time) and noted their opinion that the powders should ideally be applied to a textured surface in order that the pigments would have a key to grab onto. I was busily weathering a friend's Bachman Standard 4 at the time and once the airbrushed weathering was completed, I experimented with the rust and coal dust selection of four colours and gently applied the powders around rivet detail and other nooks and crannies using a small flattie paint brush. Only tiny amounts are required to produce the merest hint of colour variation and I was impressed with the results. My first opinions had been quite unfairly formed through lack of research. We're most of us reluctant to accept new ideas and methods of doing things if we've always done it our own way in the past – this was a prime example.

I am now quite content to use these powders to add the final touches to my

preferred painted finishes and can produce effects very similar to those created by the most expensive airbrush on very tiny areas at a time – but only when applied to a slightly textured finish. I don't feel they can take the place of the airbrush because I need that to provide the finely textured paint finish in the first place – rather they can complement the other processes for certain specialised effects. Smooth areas such as footplate edges are out of bounds because the powders are reluctant to adhere to these areas and will rub away as soon as you handle the model. I simply apply the pigments only to those parts which aren't likely to be handled or rubbed by accident. If I've applied too much powder, a water-dampened cotton bud will remove it again, so no harm's done and I can have another bash at it.

OTHER GEAR

As we go along, you will see that the decision to start weathering does not mean you *have* to go out and buy an airbrush, it just makes life a lot simpler if you own one. There are many procedures which don't use anything other than basic cheap squirrel brushes and the emphasis is on the word cheap because they will be abused quite severely during some of the more gunky stages and will be ditched after only a short time. Humbrol Senator green-handled brushes are ideal and cost around 60p each. They're not really suitable for precision painting because, particularly with the smaller ones, it may prove almost impossible

to obtain a decent tapered point. Bristles tend to come adrift after a while, which can be a little annoying if you constantly have to retrieve these wayward spikes from your paintwork, but the alternative is to use more expensive brushes and I find that difficult to live with, since they will be destroyed in use rather swiftly and I'm rather tightfisted by nature! I have never tried to hand-paint a locomotive in ex-works livery by brush, having always used an airbrush, but I imagine pure sable brushes would be the most logical choice if I had to opt for an alternative.

Flat brushes rather than pointed ones are ideal for dry brushing (we'll discuss this later) and a small selection of those made by Humbrol would be useful. Numbers 2, 4 and 6 are my favourites. A pot of Boots' own brand of cotton buds, a bottle of talcum powder (any make will suffice) a roll of paper kitchen towels plus an assortment of cocktail sticks, scalpel blades, a fibre-glass brush and any other tools which you find useful as we proceed.

Having hopefully kept you interested so far, we can get on with the show and rather than deluge you now with descriptions of all the different methods used during the various stages which follow, I think it wiser to discuss each procedure as we reach it. No doubt this will mean a certain amount of repetition, but at least this way you will become more easily familiarised with the terminology and the different procedures as they crop up.

The small shed at Hursley which I based upon a shortened version of Bude, stands deserted. Used as overnight lodgings for the branch locomotive, it would be equipped for simple maintenance and repairs.
BARRY NORMAN

STEAM LOCOMOTIVES

7mm scale short-frame 'M7' (modified DJB kit) awaiting instructions from the Hursley signalman. I used a straightforward weathering routine here for the body by duplicating the real process, airbrushing the entire loco body as described in the text, then wiping the tanks and cabsides clean with a cloth, which still leaves some residue – for example, around the two bolts on the cabside. This was followed by a delicate dusting from the airbrush to simulate fresh applications of soot and grime.

BARRY NORMAN

Without doubt, the beast at the front of the train has always held the most fascination for many, be it steam or diesel and indeed some consider the power source to be the only item of interest. Of course it is only one small part of the railway picture as a whole but, accepting that many readers may be keen to start sploshing the gunk onto their favourite loco, we may as well jump in at the deep end first.

RESEARCH AND PREPARATION

I usually rummage through several files of colour photographs in order to select the most appropriate finish for the loco concerned. This does not have to be the same class or type, just its condition – although it may be easier to create a genuine feel to the finished item if you have a photo of the actual prototype you are modelling. However, colour shots can be misleading depending upon the quality of the original slide and also, in the case of those reproduced in books, the printer's ability to interpret colours accurately. As a general guide, Kodak films have an overall blue

tint whilst others such as Agfa tend toward green and red dominant hues. Given the choice, I prefer to work from Kodak shots since many of us seem to have an affection for summertime settings for our layouts and warm, sunny days generally create a surplus of ultra violet light which adds that blue haze to the hills in the distance and also to the light reflected from the locomotives.

LIGHTING

Whilst on the subject, it's worth considering for a moment what lighting conditions will prevail when you finally sit back and admire your models, because the type of light blazing down upon your creation will dictate which of the colours you choose to dominate in your weathering mixes. Let me explain.

Most domestic interior lighting generates an overall yellowish warm tint and is perfect for creating a welcoming light in the home, but for illuminating models it can entirely change the colour of a shade of paint by artificially adding yellow to the tone. When this is reflected back, you sud-

denly find that particular colour which you spent ages trying to match perfectly with your photographs has suddenly altered completely. This is simply because the prototype was photographed outside in daylight which is usually blue dominant. Try the test for yourself by taking your model outdoors on a bright day and see the colours change. If you propose keeping your models illuminated by domestic light, you will need either to add more blue to your paint in order to compensate for the yellow light, or add extra blue spotlights or special blue daylight strip-lights to your lighting set-up and you will be free to copy your prototype colouring without undue concern.

Now this does mean that where you choose to carry out your painting will require some thought, and I try to paint my models only during the day where strong daylight bears down upon my work. I also use an Anglepoise lamp which has a Crompton Craft light bulb fitted (available from Howes of Oxford) and this simulates natural daylight. Similarly, when spraying,

At first glance this L & Y 4-4-0 looks pretty clean until you look close and see the tender sides, streaked with delicate stains, the connecting rods dull instead of shiny and there are other smears and blemishes lurking in crevices and gulleys.
LENS OF SUTTON

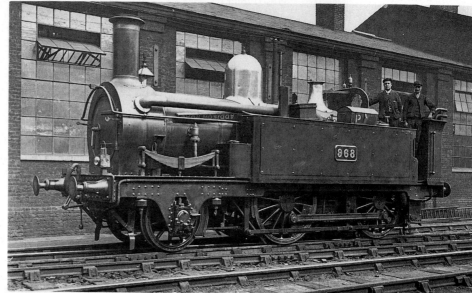

An early photograph of a 'Metro' Class 2-4-0T No. 968 in fairly immaculate order — or is it?

Delicate lining adds grace to an elegant shape. Although clean, there are patches of dust still adhering. The handrails are not glaringly bright despite being unpainted.
H. J. STRETTON-WARD

Finally in place on its siding, the illusion is almost achieved. Scale couplings and front steps would clinch it, though.

ened paint (because it adheres much more firmly to the glue than the bare rims) and certainly shouldn't remove the glue beneath. This really is a last ditch stand and if you're at all bothered about using superglue anywhere near valve gear and other such paraphernalia, then this may not be the answer to all your dreams.

Apart from the addition of any extra hand rails, scale couplings or any other fittings which you feel inclined to provide, the model should be ready for the weathering to take place.

'J94' — almost clean wheels — but look behind. The spring is coated with gunge.

THE WEATHERING (at last!)

Traditionally, it is accepted that only in the last desperate days of steam would one see locomotives looking really filthy yet there are many hundreds of photographs taken well back into the early parts of this century which prove otherwise. However, it is certainly true that when the approaching demise of steam was officially declared, the heart seemed to go out of the crews so that locomotives were allowed to become prematurely corroded and filthy as if anticipating their imminent passing. Prior to this, cleaning staff were freely available and the motion would normally be kept well oiled and maintained. However, the bits behind the wheels seldom received much more than a glance and therefore became pretty silted up over a period of time.

Study this area of a locomotive's underframe in close detail and you will observe that the colours are many and varied but with hardly a hint of pure black in sight. These assorted colours appear almost at random with oily blue shiny patches amidst an overall build-up of thick dirt and grime. Wonderful!

As a general guide, I use matt enamel paints for the weathering unless otherwise

Axlebox with bubbling and peeling paint, highlights and shadows, plus an oily sheen. Delightful!
P. SIMPSON

Lining is subdued and often finer than most modellers think.
H. J. STRETTON-WARD

Buffer beam lining may be impossible with a bow pen or lining pen so transfers may be the only option.
H. J. STRETTON-WARD

Two fine shots — the upper, taken in 1938, shows this Great Central 4–6–0 acceptably clean but with a fairly flat uniform appearance. The airbrush will accomplish this with ease. The lower view shows the same engine (in July 1937) with the paintwork polished up with oil. Although considerably improved, the enlivened result still shows the grime trapped about the handrail knobs and along the piping runs, and on the smokebox. The boiler has that elusive oil sheen — achievable by polishing the paintwork with a nylon mop in a modelling drill.

H. E. SIMMONS

No. 453, photographed at Waterloo in 1939, appears fairly immaculate. Subtle light weathering would be necessary if emulating this fine example.

H. E. SIMMONS

Smears, scratches, chips, dents, dribbles, puddles and runs remind us that these beasts are alive.
G. PLATT

Lulworth Castle, with low tender, seems fairly clean but the cab roof has a matt finish and the cylinder cover is stained along with the smokebox door. Patches of grime can just be discerned on the wheel rims and about the brake blocks. The rims are not polished chrome, neither are the rods.

H. J. STRETTON-WARD

No. 5069 looking smart, but peer more closely at the blemishes and stains present in abundance, the oil stains on the rims in line with each spoke. The paintwork is faded and the lining almost obscured with a fine dust coating, but the rods are quite clean.

H. J. STRETTON-WARD

stipulated, selected from the following: Black (33), Leather (62), Orange (82), Gunmetal (53), Grey (64) and Tarmac (112). Tarmac has a blue/grey colouring which is a more subtle way of providing a ready mixed artificial blue tint (pretty good for roof slates of the blue/grey variety). I also employ Bauxite (133) (or Red Leather in the J.P. range), both of which are semi-matt.

I make fairly extensive use of Humbrol 'Metalcote' enamels, in particular the 'Gunmetal' which creates a dark black/blue finish and can be polished gently, producing a fine sheen. This will prove useful as we go along.

So take your brush and enamels and, referring constantly to your colour photographs, apply as many of these colours as

you wish to the chassis, blending them into one another whilst wet in a stippling action and at the same time adding copious amounts of talcum powder by also stippling this into the paint. For those of you who aren't sure, 'stippling' is a sort of short stabbing action with the brush. This addition of the talc not only creates a textured finish, but it also acts as a matting agent to the

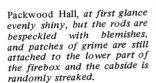

Packwood Hall, *at first glance evenly shiny, but the rods are bespeckled with blemishes, and patches of grime are still attached to the lower part of the firebox and the cabside is randomly streaked.*

A 1931 photo to complete the quartet. Highly polished but the smokebox has flattened off, probably because of heat, creating a contrast to the boiler. The front footplate is patchy as well.
H. J. STRETTON-WARD

The '61XX' was to be weathered using this prototype example as a guide.   S. H. FREESE

paint – although a hint of oily shine here and there is quite useful.

I'm inclined to use Gunmetal/Bauxite/Orange combined to simulate a rusty sludge colour, varying the proportions as I go along the underframe and adding in the occasional tiny blob of Leather (62) whilst observing the colours in the photographs as closely as possible. Feel free to build up the texture until a really good gunk is in place. This should then be left to dry for an hour or so and in the meantime, work can commence on the bodywork.

You will notice that your paintbrushes look more like chimney sweep brushes now and should be thoroughly cleaned of all paint and talcum powder, dried on a cloth and put to one side. They won't last very long anyway, but every effort helps.

For the bodywork, again study your selected photographs and observe the subtle variations in colour. Although you may initially think of the loco as black, your eyes will soon pick out the tremendous contrasts from a shiny blue/black through shades of grey and into quite vivid oranges in the really rusty parts.

To the task in hand, then, and we can mix enamel paint in the ratio of 2 parts Metalcote Gunmetal, 1 part Tarmac (112) and 1 part Leather (62) – the latter is an optional colour addition to give that slight brownish tint which may be observed on the real thing under some lighting con-

The business end of Tony's superb model which I have, hopefully, enhanced with my own contributions.   TONY SMITH

ditions – it all depends upon the evidence in your photographs. If the locomotive is to be only lightly weathered, this mix should be gently sprayed over the loco body sufficiently just to tone down the paintwork and show a build-up of soot on the upper surfaces of the boiler and cab roof. Slightly denser coatings may be applied into the corners and other areas where appropriate. The lining and company emblems should now appear somewhat less distinct than when originally applied. Vary the mixtures of colour as you go along by increasing the Gunmetal or adding more Leather. The sheen of the locomotive's body colour will

still 'grin' through the haze (provided you haven't sprayed the whole thing with matt varnish beforehand!). The footplate can be treated to reasonably heavy coatings since these parts were seldom given much attention even when in for overhaul.

Clean the airbrush by spraying neat *cellulose* thinners through it onto a scrap of paper until no trace of colour shows. Now spray light coatings of leather/orange in a 50/50 mix onto those patchy areas which appear rusty according to the photograph you are working from. Add brighter tones where you want signs of fresher rust showing through the grime. Don't try to imagine

these shadings, paint what you see – not what you think you see (remember the motto?).

If you haven't an airbrush, it is possible to very gently stipple these colours onto your model using a 'flattie' brush although it is not so easy to apply a hazing effect over numbers or lettering. If the finish required is fairly hefty abuse, then stippling can be extremely effective. Gunmetal (53) has metallic particles in its content which produces a most authentic dusty finish to the paintwork and creates an added texture to the surface. You can now put the body to one side to dry for at least six hours.

Weathered to look smart and well cared for but with evidence of soot and dust in abundance.

My attempts at weathering the underframe of Tony Reynalds' 7mm scale model of a '61XX', much as described in the text.

A '55XX' looking typical of its ilk. The rivets and running plate edges are highlighted by the bright daylight and the loco can hardly be described as filthy. However, the tank sides are dirtier than might at first be assumed. The company name is slowly fading into the dust.
H. J. STRETTON-WARD

Returning to the underframe, work can commence on the connecting rods and if they are in their natural unprimed state, a simple oily sheen may be all you are looking for. To achieve this, mix *gloss* tan (No. 9) with a small amount of 'polished steel' from the Humbrol 'Metalcote' range and apply this in well diluted form to the motion. This should leave that yellowy oiled effect. If applied over the black primed rods, a similar but darker effect will result and this can be further enhanced by an airbrushed application of the standard weathering mix.

The wheels can either be finished in a relatively clean state or be given the paint and talc treatment, indicating lack of maintenance in a similar manner to the frames behind them. The Humbrol Metalcote 'Gunmetal' (not to be confused with normal Gunmetal No. 53) can be applied to the spokes, and when dry, polished gently with a cotton bud. This, to represent freshly applied paint, gives a more natural metallic appearance than the gloss blacks commonly employed. For wheels which appear tarnished rather than dirty, then Gunmetal (53) can be utilised instead.

The frames and wheels will now have an overall murky appearance but will

somehow be lacking in life and reality. A real locomotive is large, and with the bright light of day bearing down upon it, all the edges, angles and fine details are highlighted accordingly. Due to its diminutive size in comparison, a model locomotive can only appear so if you shine a really bright light

upon it, which will probably neither be practical nor even desirable. You need to create these highlights and shadows artificially and here we come to the art of 'drybrushing'. This is one of those terms frequently referred to in modelling articles but which seldom carries an accompanying

By weathering and highlighting the '61XX's underframe, the quality of Tony's constructional skills is emphasised rather than being lost amidst the original gloss black paint.

The Malcolm Mitchell '44XX' ready for work. To achieve the mottled effect was very simple. One hour after spraying with the weathering mix, I gently rubbed a thumb in vertical motion down the tank sides. This removed part of the coating only. Particularly noticeable is the grime trapped around the rivet detail. A partial extra dusting was applied and all left to dry. Handling the loco will probably improve the finish as time goes by.

The sunlight reflections exaggerate the mottled effect on the tank sides of Malcolm's '44XX' quite convincingly.

explanation. For those of you who already know about these things, bear with me.

Drybrushing simply means loading the paintbrush with paint, wiping the bristles over a cloth until nearly all of the paint has gone and then gently rubbing or flicking the almost 'dry' brush over any raised detail on the model. This will cause tiny deposits of the paint still remaining in the brush to be attached to the bumps in the paintwork and thus create a three-dimensional contrasting effect by highlighting all the raised parts. The keyword here is 'restraint'. Overdo the drybrushing and the model may take on the appearance of something that's been blitzed by an incontinent bullock. Not nice. Be subtle with your work – better to slightly understate the effects than over-emphasise them.

So, in the case of the rusty sludge on the frames, by *delicately* drybrushing over the textured surfaces with lighter shades of the sludge colour, the murky parts will start to come to life before your very eyes. Use a small 'flattie' brush for drybrushing rather than a normal pointed type as this offers better control of the effect.

For some reason, mixing 'Metalcote Gunmetal' with light grey (64) in approximately 4:1 ratio gives a convincing blue/black oily sheen to the paintwork when drybrushed over oil boxes, diesel loco bogie frames, or wherever oil gathers. I don't know why this should be, but perhaps

No. 5538 in rather decrepit state – and not in BR days – the letters are still visible. Lots of scratches, chalk inscriptions and streaks in the dust. The only clean parts are the handrails and the areas around them which have been polished as a result of handling by the crew.

L. E. COPELAND

The paintwork around the spectacle plates is pretty grim with the top coat chipped and flaking away. G. PLATT

The same loco with smokebox and dome to match. Stippling in talcum powder whilst painting these areas by hand would simulate these effects. The rivets and bolts on the buffer beam have tiny circles of dirt surrounding them. Drybrush all of the above to highlight the raised detail.

G. PLATT

No. 8253 is fairly clean overall but the running board has footprints clearly visible in the ash.

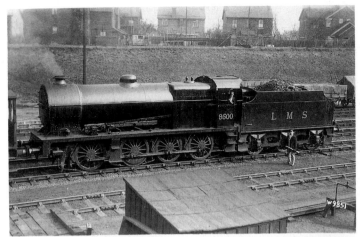

Top: *No. 9500 — spotless black? Not quite. Study closer and you will see the vertical staining of fresh activity forming. The underframe is positively filthy.* Centre: *No. 8914 — the more familiar condition of the freight locomotive, faded black with an even coating of grime, and rivets and boiler bands emphasised with darker shades. The running plate shows evidence of oil, water and ash disturbed by the crew's size 9's.* Above: *No. 7354 is relatively tidy. Note all the delicate streaks and dribbles running vertically, not horizontally.*   L. E. COPELAND and LENS OF SUTTON

Brassmasters 4mm scale 'Black 5' weathered in typical freight-hauling condition. Rivets are highlighted by dry-brushing with lighter shades of the overall colours. Without this, the detail could not be easily observed.   TONY SMITH

Three more views of the 'Black Five'. Only the airbrush can satisfactorily provide a fine dusted finish. Once dry, the highlighting can take place, either by polishing the raised detail, or by drybrushing with lighter shades of the same colours. Talcum powder brushed over the entire loco should add a subtle sparkle to the paintwork.
TONY SMITH and AUTHOR

This was approximately the condition desired by Tony's customer and I therefore weathered the '61XX' accordingly as the photo below illustrates.

original colours in cellulose or at least protecting the enamels (if originally used) with acrylic varnish. No matter how many times you use the enamel thinners, the basic body colour remains undamaged. Once again, a final light hazy dusting from the airbrush will indicate the loco, although relatively clean, is still alive and kicking out smoke and soot.

Once dry, the footplate which has remained coated in the various grimy mixes can be gently brushed and lightly scrubbed in all directions with a dry, stubby, clean brush which will have the effect of scuffing the surface indicating where the crew have clambered about and disturbed the grime. This action will also lightly polish any raised rivet detail, etc, which will highlight those areas. Lamp irons, handrails and any sharp edges can be gently scrubbed or, using lighter shades of the sooty mix, drybrushed to highlight them accordingly.

Where you wish to simulate rust or dust gathering about the rivets, once you are certain the paintwork has completely dried and has had time to harden, gently wash thinners over the desired areas and whilst still wet, just barely touch the raised rivets with a small brush loaded with the rust colour of your choice. Try a yellowish orange for the fresh rust look [Orange (82) and Leather (62)]. This 'rust' will be drawn around the detail by capillary action and tiny rust rings will result when all is dry. If you wish to present your loco in really abused condition, stipple Gunmetal (53) and a slight hint of Bauxite (133) over most of the bodywork and when this has dried, drybrush the surfaces to produce all the

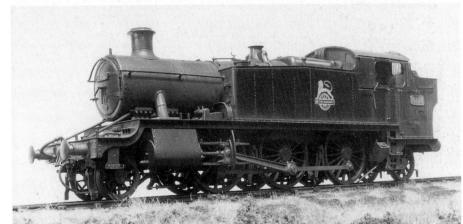

Left: *As supplied — an exquisite model.* Right: *Restrained weathering has, hopefully, produced an illusion of reality.*

A different angle this time, with dust gathering about the rivets plus smears and scuffs from the 'human' touch.

Using Gunmetal (53) and small touches of Bauxite (180), the paintwork takes on a more convincing metallic feel.

variety of highlights shown in your photographs.

In some cases, the smokebox shows signs of intense heat and some of the top coat paint will have flaked away exposing rusty patches beneath. To represent this, observe from your photographs exactly where these patches appear and paint the tiny areas with your by now favourite rusty concoction – again by stippling plus the addition of talcum powder. When these patches have completely dried, protect them by applying small blobs of Humbrol Maskol which is a pink rubbery solution sold in most model shops. You can apply this either with a small brush or cocktail stick. The Maskol is water soluble whilst wet so that you can clean your brush easily, but after it has dried (which is fairly swiftly), you will need to use white spirit or enamel thinners to dissolve the rubbery material.

White PVA glue would be an alternative to the Maskol but it won't dry nearly so quickly. Once the Maskol has dried, paint the entire area with your selected smokebox weathering mix and again leave to dry. You

should now have a very lumpy looking smokebox! Don't worry, that's how it's supposed to look at this stage. Now take a pair of tweezers and gently pluck the Maskol pieces from the model. If everything has gone to plan, these expose the rust beneath with the topcoat flaking at the edges. Gently rub a finger across the surfaces which should remove any chippings of paint and you will hopefully see a fairly convincing version of your photographed example.

Buffer heads usually show in photographs as being polished in the centre which is either because they are (!) or because they have recently been greased to reduce friction. To simulate this, you can either paint the heads in 'Metalcote Polished Steel' or 'Gunmetal' and then physically buff up the centres with a dry cotton bud, or use a soft pencil and create the 'polished' look with the lead. You may feel that the overall airbrushed weathered finish is too uniform and your photographs may show evidence of added scuffs, grazes or smears on the bodywork. These are simulated by

physically scuffing, grazing or smearing the paint with a dry cotton bud or flattened-off cocktail stick until the appearance duplicates that of your photograph. Vertical stains or streaks of colour may be added using a very fine brush but be careful not to overdo these as they can look far too contrived. Tone them down with the airbrush or subtle stippling at the edges of the streaks to reduce the contrast. Water spillage is created by using very thin applications of gloss varnish with a small brush.

If you wish to add further colour shading changes, now should be a good time to use Carr's weathering powders on those areas which are textured, such as underframes, smokebox, etc – particularly if the areas concerned are difficult to get at with an airbrush (behind wheels for example). Also, as mentioned in the earlier section dealing with these powders, it may be simpler to use them for the tiniest of areas where an airbrush, stippling or drybrushing may just be too much like hard work! The powdered pigments are quickly applied with no drying time involved.

Left: *Before – with shiny copper, couplings and buffer heads, also matt black smokebox.* Right: *After – Chemical blackening of the shiny metal plus polishing of the smokebox door create a more realistic appearance. Airbrushing and drybrushing add further dimensions to the overall effect.*

A Southern quartet. No. 743 looks reasonable although obviously not clean. The headcode discs are seldom pure white.

H. J. STRETTON-WARD

No. 30453 looks evenly weathered with just a solitary dribble from the draincock and a subtle streak or two to disturb the dusty coating.

No. 31794 — a 7mm scale DJB kit coming off shed at Hursley, her lining almost obscured under a coating of grime.   BARRY NORMAN

Many hours can be spent adding extra fine touches and it is sometimes a good idea to put the loco away in a box and return to it several days later. This gives your brain a rest and allows you to review your work with a clear mind, enabling you to spot any areas which somehow don't seem to be convincing.

Experiment by finally lightly dusting some of the surfaces with small amounts of talcum powder applied with a soft, dry, clean brush. This has a twofold effect: it reduces the contrast in colours and at the same time adds a subtle sparkle to the paint-work, further enhancing the overall picture.

OTHER LIVERIES

For locomotives painted other than black, a little more experimentation will have to be carried out, depending upon the livery concerned. As a general rule, if I'm painting a specific colour, I rarely use exactly the shade as indicated in the pot. Colours frequently appear a tone or two lighter when

No. 30453 again, with dents in her cylinder cover and irregular smears on her smoke deflector, probably rubbed on by the engineman's sleeve as he edged by. Note the polished area where the crosshead slippers constantly rub.

7mm scale 'B4' No. 30096, mostly scratchbuilt plus a few parts from a Vulcan kit, portrayed in final form before being sold into private use. The prototype now works regularly on the Bluebell line but in her early LSWR guise. She is weathered much as I remember her at Winchester in the 'sixties.

Left & below: *7mm scale 'M7' Class 0—4—4T No. 30249 at Hursley, seen from above, showing boiler, cab roof and other horizontal surfaces attracting all the grime whilst the sides are relatively clean. The second photo compares favourably with 'O2' No. 30225 seen at Bere, Alston, for similar weathering effects.* AUTHOR and ROGER CARPENTER

seen at normal viewing distances, but it's not just a case of adding white to the paint because this may not have the required effect. It will lighten it, but won't actually change its colour content, whereas if the paintwork of the prototype has been faded by the sun over a period of time, it's often only the darker pigment which has been attacked. For example, take green which at its simplest is just blue and yellow. Sunlight fades blue very quickly and therefore green becomes more yellowy as the blue is decreased. To simulate this, just add extra yellow to your green mix and you will be able to reproduce the effect for yourself. You are actually altering the colour rather than simply lightening it.

If in doubt concerning the pigments involved, a return visit to your friendly car paint shop will enable you to look through the colour swatches where most shades are classified by the British Standards system of numbering we discussed earlier. Find the colour patch which is nearest to it and it should tell you how many parts of each pigment must be combined in order to create that colour. In so doing, this will also explain which of the lighter colours in that mixture will require increasing in proportion to the others so that your faded paint finish can be realised. The problem here is that we're getting a bit bogged down with science again, and researching which of the component parts of any colour scheme are or are not affected by sunlight or intense heat and to what degree is possibly not on your list of priorities — nor

BARRY NORMAN

probably should it be. I suspect life will be much simpler if you just slightly lighten the basic paint colour and blend that in where appropriate. Artificial shadows can be sprayed in using a darker body shade.

Wheels and underframes may have been painted in fairly bright colours and possibly lined as well. Unless you require a heavily weathered result, the airbrush really comes into its own here by enabling you to add subtle dustings of paint which will tone down the colours without obscuring the original finish underneath. As a final touch to obtain a polished but worn appearance, perhaps after spraying the body colour with just a light weathering mix (which may leave the paintwork looking a little flat and uninteresting), take a polishing mop in your small Expo electric drill, or whatever you use for such purposes, and gently buff up the paintwork. This can, with a little care, simulate that sheen on the paint where the oily rag has been lovingly applied.

'Q1' No. 33020, another 7mm scale model from a DJB kit, simmering outside Hursley signal cabin — ugly but very powerful and with typical weathered appearance. Airbrush to the fore for these blendings of shade.

DIESELS

If tin boxes are your preference, many of the procedures already discussed are appropriate. For a cleanish look, the same basic rules apply as for steam outline models, but, when it comes to partly removing the weathering along the sides and ends, use the cotton bud in an up and down motion only. That way, all streaks of residue will be in vertical lines following the laws of gravity.

Grilles and louvres may be highlighted using the drybrush technique, perhaps using neat 'Steel' to indicate paint having chipped or flaked away from the sharp edges. Spray roofs using a mix of Metalcote Gunmetal and Leather, increasing the blackening effect around grilles and exhaust ports by adding more Gunmetal. I used to use Matt Black (33) with the Leather (62) but the end result was too flat a finish, but by using the Metalcote Gunmetal, the paint is physically polished gently with a finger once dry, which will add extra sheen to the surface and highlight the roof rivets, bolt heads etc. Again, the Metalcote 'Gunmetal' is very effective with the slight addition of grey to produce oily streaks or patches. In the case of commercially made diesel models, unless you are stripping the factory finish and starting from scratch with a new paint job, you are obliged to resort to cos-

metic treatment of the existing paintwork to simulate the effects you require.

Drybrush vertically the entire sides and ends with random blendings of lighter and darker shades of the topcoat colour, to represent the fading and streaking of the paint,

Two views of a Ruston diesel shunter constructed from an Impetus 7mm kit.

assuming you require a really dilapidated appearance. When this has dried and fully hardened, you might abuse it further by applying very fine applications of Daywat Liquid Poly to the paint. This will bubble the paint by attacking the varnish and enamel content, and should be left to harden again.

Fainter staining may be desired and Mek-Pak applied with a cotton bud, (once again in vertical rubbing motions) will, being less potent than DayWat, wear away the paint without bubbling it and, incidentally, can be used to flatten or create a more matt finish on painted surfaces which may have become too shiny.

Variations in shade of the stained areas are more effectively produced by vertical fine sprayings from your airbrush, blending in lighter and darker tints of the topcoat colour, plus slight oily or rusty stainings (see the photographs of the Ruston Diesel for these effects).

Underframe treatment is much the same as that of the steam locos, although there is usually more evidence of brake dust build-up with diesels. Matt Leather/Orange should suffice sprayed from the airbrush or just stippled onto the chassis by brush. More drybrushing with lighter shades will highlight all of the cables and ancillary equip-

No. 10001 looking purposeful in lined black and hauling a mixed freight on 25th March 1950. The grey roof and bogies were already acquiring some signs of use and a light build-up of dust elsewhere.

E. D. BRUTON/NRM

ment which abounds on the bogies, and the Metalcote Gunmetal/Light Grey mix will again emphasise the oily content of some of the gunk and grime which has adhered to the bogies.

Returning to the bodywork, the bubbled paintwork can either be left as it is and then highlighted by drybrushing with lighter shades of the body colour to emphasise the raised detail, or even further abused by gently scrubbing with a fibreglass brush, or with fine emery paper in vertical motions. This will flake away the raised edges of the bubbled paint and expose the base colour underneath. Be careful here as many commercial diesel models are made from yellow plastic so that the ends don't have to be painted in the factory and if you scrub too hard, you will expose yellow areas under the topcoat which will look a little unusual to say the least. Gently done, the effort will reward you with a realistic faded paint effect.

An alternative method is to use enamel thinners on a cotton bud and wipe the surface of the paint repeatedly in an up and down action until the paint becomes faded

Typical condition for a blue era locomotive — blue has always been notorious for fading.

*Initial treament of No. 47006 with bogies sprayed,
the roof toned down and faint streaks of grime descending
from roof line to simulate exhaust deposits plus general traffic grime.*

through constant wear. Using the same action, but with a fibreglass brush, will produce a similar effect but with a slightly rougher texture.

If you intend to show the loco as being in sound painted condition but with traffic grime attached, the sides can be given a dusting from the airbrush to simulate the build-up of grime, perhaps with heavier applications of the Black/Leather tones on the lower areas, fading into almost no dusting toward the upper parts of the body. Where oil and diesel exhaust deposits have built up in certain areas, use the airbrush to apply vertical bands of Leather/Metalcote Gunmetal mixed together. It is important for these streams or bands of paint to have soft edges fading into the surrounding areas, and a quality airbrush will achieve this with ease. Alternatively, spraying through a hole in a piece of paper with the airbrush held about half an inch away from the surface of the paper and the paper the same distance from the model, you will reduce the chance of harsh edges being formed, which is useful if your airbrush is of the less expensive type without the finer spraying abilities. When dry, very gently rub the 'oil' patches with a finger, which will result in an oily sheen rather than a matt finish.

Roof grilles and meshes painted in the darker weathering tones and then drybrushed with a lighter shade will highlight the detail. This drybrushing should be carried out on all the locomotive's raised bits which will bring everything to life rather than appearing somewhat drab and

Drybrushing of louvres and grilles with lighter shades brings them to life, as seen on these Lima examples.

Top left & right: *Two model photos showing how removing the weathering with vertical actions will leave a residue of streaks, lending further character to an otherwise flat area. Prototype photos:* Centre left: *Relatively clean, but the lower bodysides remain filthy.* Centre right: *No. 47829 on shed with light spatterings showing on her cab front. Try using the airbrush incorrectly, i.e. allow a little paint flow before the air flow and you should produce tiny spits and spats. Note the greased buffer heads.* Bottom left: *No. 47152 inside Laira shed with paintwork chipping and vertical streaks.* Bottom centre: *A Class 50 showing very subtle delicate streaks with one pronounced line trailing down from the rain strip. Note the highlighted louvre edges.*

The two shots on this page show that almost without exception, the stains, dribbles and faded areas have a vertical action — simple laws of gravity.

too uniform as a result of the overall spraying.

If you require an appearance of a recent visit to the diesel 'car-wash', then after weathering the sides, leave the loco to dry for several hours or, even better, leave it for two or three days and then take an enamel thinners-moistened cotton bud and gently rub the sides vertically from top to bottom so that the airbrushed weathering starts to come away. In the case of 4 mm Lima locos, the factory paint finish has a slightly porous quality to it which under normal circumstances would be considered less than ideal. However, from our point of view, this is rather a bonus because it is almost impossible to completely remove the weathering no matter how vigorous you are with the thinners and this leaves a most realistic impression of stained paintwork.

The Lima '47' and '31' are as purchased, but after weathering look just that bit more convincing, I feel.

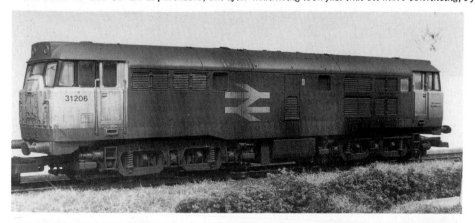

Alternatively, to create finer delicate traces of vertical streaking, don't leave the paint to dry for so long (next day at the latest) before taking a flattie brush (No. 2 or 4) and using the thinners again, gently rub the bristles from top to bottom so that the weathering will come away in finer streaks. Make sure that this vertical action is precisely that, because if the brushing action is at odd angles, the overall impression will look unnatural and lose its realism. If you've waited too long after spraying the sides, the paint will have hardened beyond the point where the flattie brush and thinners will be able to have any effect without more vigorous scrubbing, and this can create its own problems if you're not wary.

You may either leave the loco as it is, or perhaps offer a final misting of traffic grime from the airbrush combining, say, Matt Black (No. 33) and Leather (No. 62) just sufficient to tone down the whole effect. Make sure the wheel treads are clean and your loco can burble its way into service on your layout.

If you've decided to have a bash yourself, I would suggest you practise on an old, less cherished model or just on odd scraps of plasticard or brass until you're happy with the results.

The texture of the Lima factory finish can easily be discerned here.

PASSENGER STOCK

D. CLAYTON

Once you have weathered your first loco, the stock riding behind it will stand out like several sore thumbs because it will look far too squeaky clean. Carriages are somewhat easier to weather because they don't emit any nasty smoke or fumes by themselves. However, they do suffer the ravages of rain and sun and are 'passive smokers', collecting the soot and grime which is carried from the locomotive to their nice clean paintwork by the wind and gravity. As a general rule, the sides are kept pretty clean since they are intended to be attractive to paying passengers, but the underframes and roofs are a different story. Out of sight, out of mind, perhaps. The underframes would only be cleaned prior to painting when overhauled and the roofs would often be ignored unless repairs were deemed necessary. Underneath detail can be treated as already described, but the roofs should be given further consideration due to the nature of the materials employed in their manufacture.

Some early coaching stock was turned out with white roofs but these toned down pretty quickly in traffic and a lighter shade of the weathering mix can be sprayed over the surface. Other stock would have timber roofs covered in canvas and on Maunsell Southern coaches (which my father helped construct at the Eastleigh carriage works), this canvas would then have several coats of boiled linseed oil swabbed onto it with large mops. This would seal the canvas and when dry, the roof would be painted with a grey paint as an added waterproofer and to provide a smart appearance. On hot days, the linseed oil would bubble up underneath the paint and form a sticky goo which would then attract all the soot and grime, acting like a horizontal flypaper. One way to presented this effect is to spray the roof with the weathering mix of your choice and, when dry, take a small brush and apply neat thinners or Mek-Pak by just touching the rainstrip or base of the ventilators with the tip so that the fluids will run into the channels and along the rainstrip by capillary action. This should leave staining patches in natural positions. To create a heavier effect, the Day-Wat can again be used to bubble the paint by sparingly applying by brush to small patches of these stained parts which will simulate the more drastic sludge-like appearance.

Incidentally, at most of these fiddly stages, if you get it wrong, you're unlikely to cause much grief to the overall appearance unless you've perhaps spilled the entire contents of a bottle of Day-Wat over the roof. Then you may have to re-paint the roof, but, being naturally grubby, it will not look too odd if you have made a botch of perhaps just one part and are wondering what to do next. Just take the faithful airbrush or stippling brush and disguise any minor errors with another coating of gunk. However, most of the chemicals react quite slowly and you have time to neutralise them if you're not happy with what is happening. If you use small quantities at a time, you run less risk of terminal damage being inflicted – talking of which, I must add the following warning: when you are using chemicals such as Day-Wat, be aware of their toxic nature. Most have quite a pungent smell which alone should tell you

This 1947 photo, taken at Bedford St. John's, shows a passenger train whose loco and coaches appear to have been 'airbrushed' together since they bear an even coating of dust. The chimney and smokebox had got a little hot at some time, judging by the peeling paint.

W. A. CAMWELL

not to breathe the fumes, but under no circumstances should you smoke when using them. It can be fatal.

Some coaches have metal roofs and these have seam lines at regular intervals spanning the width which attract darker shades of traffic grime. Once you've completed the roof's basic weathering and when you're certain all is dry, run a gentle wash of thinners over the entire roof surface and touch the seams with a brush dipped in a very dark oily shade such as the Metalcote Gunmetal. You are, in effect forming shadows in the grooves which should show up quite subtly when everything has dried off. Similarly, with metal roofed stock, paint does seem to come away from the metal in flaking patches – but only in isolated cases. I've yet to establish quite why this is, but if you wanted to reproduce the effect, then the Maskol routine might fit the bill.

The coach ends can be sprayed with the usual weathering mix, and subsequent

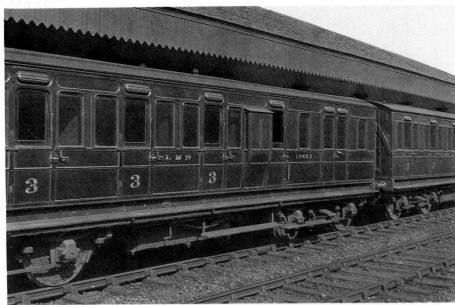

The underframes in these two pictures are grubby but the panelled sides are rather smart. Look closely, however, and you will see the remnants of dust trapped amongst the raised detail.
H. J. STRETTON-WARD and G. PLATT

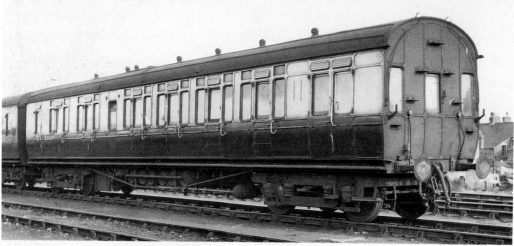

An assortment of panelled stock, some of which look pristine until closer study reveals a multitude of weathered effects. The photo at the bottom here and the one at the top of the opposite page show evidence of particular staining patterns in the upper panels, whilst the centre photo opposite illustrates distinct contrasts with almost a 'before and after' effect with the two sharing a siding. Even so, the underframes and buffer heads of the recently outshopped pair are quite grubby. The final photo pictures a duo with fine streaks in the lower panels beneath a top coat of dust. The roofs are matt grime.

J. H. RUSSELL,
ROYE ENGLAND and
J. F. RUSSELL SMITH

No. 5621 at the head of the Anglo Scottish Express departing from St. Pancras on 11th August 1935. The coach roofs have a sooty coating with a textured content, as do the underframes, whilst the teak sides have grime trapped in the seams and about the hinges.
J. H. L. ADAMS

coats, using more Leather (62) content and less Black (33), may be blended in by grading from the bottom up toward the roofline. Good photographs are again essential here as no two coaches are alike. The sides should be lightly dusted and then the weathering removed again, using thinners and cotton buds, leaving dusty deposits in the door seams, around hinges and behind door and grab handles where the cleaners have been unable to go. If you wish to get in behind any of these obstructions, refer to the earlier section dealing with the cleaning of locomotives.

Protect glazing either with masking tape or with Humbrol Maskol which can be peeled off afterwards. If you really want clean windows, then the glazing should ideally be removed or in the case of a kit, not have been installed yet. If you require windows which have become dirty and then cleaned, first of all experiment with a spare piece of glazing material to establish whether your thinners will damage it or not. Some glazing goes milky and there is nothing to be done but replace it, so test it first to be sure.

Once the coach has been sprayed, take a cotton bud and gently wash the weathering from the windows, followed by a final cleaning with a dry cotton bud. Some of the weathering residue will become trapped in

The numbers on this teak coach are subdued yet still visible beneath a haze of dust.
ROYE ENGLAND

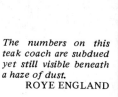

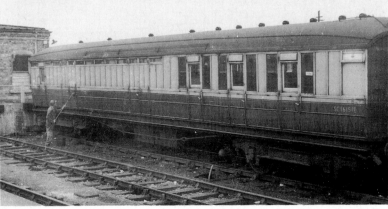

Peeling paint exposing the teak beneath the BR crimson and cream livery, while trapped grime creates false shadows in the panels. The final picture in this detailed study of a Gresley brake shows cleaning the hard way which we can duplicate with the cotton bud and thinners system with similar results. ROYE ENGLAND

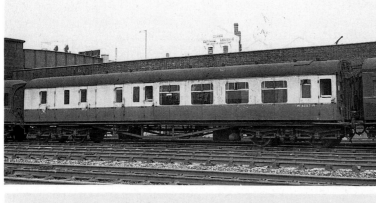

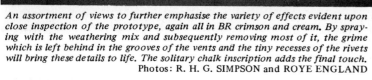

An assortment of views to further emphasise the variety of effects evident upon close inspection of the prototype, again all in BR crimson and cream. By spraying with the weathering mix and subsequently removing most of it, the grime which is left behind in the grooves of the vents and the tiny recesses of the rivets will bring these details to life. The solitary chalk inscription adds the final touch.
Photos: R. H. G. SIMPSON and ROYE ENGLAND

Puckers and dents in the panels add character to a flush-sided coach.

R. H. G. SIMPSON

A 7mm scale model of Southern Region BR Push/Pull coach from an RJH kit with much additional detail and photographed at Hursley station awaiting the Motorman's return. Smart green paintwork but the uneven reflections along the side betray the realistic distortions in the apparently thin metal. The small gatherings of dust trapped in the rivet recesses lend depth to what might otherwise be a rather mundane front end.

BARRY NORMAN

GUVs in service but with peeling roofs, encroaching rust and those softly blended-in stains running top to bottom apart from a small pattern blown along the side by the wind. The eye is drawn to the hinges by the grime surrounding each one.

the nooks and crannies around the windows which will add to the effect. If you prefer your coaches to be a little more unkempt, then spraying the sides, graduating from heavier to lighter as you progress from bottom to top, will indicate fairly heavy traffic use. Parcels stock seldom appears to have its windows cleaned, probably because there are no passengers demanding to see out of them and you will be able to spray the sides in a fairly heavy coating without having to worry about the glazing. Most photographs show evidence of the sticky finger brigade – i.e. graffiti, and it is very simple to represent this after the weathering has dried. Simply sharpen a cocktail stick and gently scribe your chosen words into

The paint has bubbled here and is peeling back, revealing the metal roof beneath.

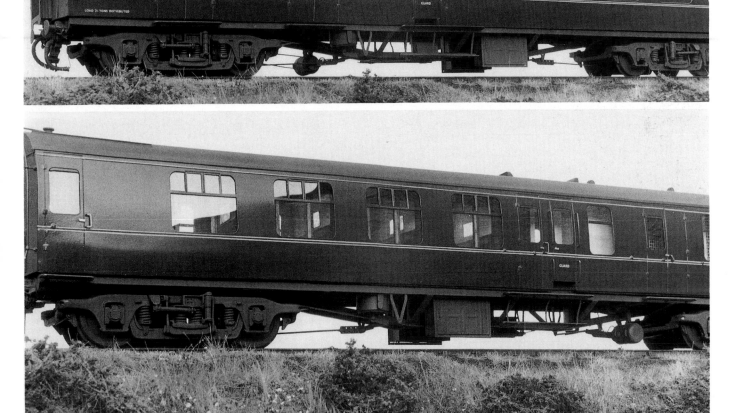

This 7mm scale BR Mk I came from from another RJH kit constructed by Geoff Grayson. I have painted, lined and weathered this example much as per the Gresley coach overleaf, cleaning off sides leaving deposits in door seams and around hinges. The ends, underframe and roof are airbrushed with varying shades of Leather (62) and Matt Black (33). The bogie springs are drybrushed with the polished Metalcote Gunmetal to simulate an oily sheen.

the weathered areas of the sides or windows so that clean paint or glazing shows underneath – just like the real thing. Treat the cocktail stick as an imagined finger. Although it's been sharpened, it's still relatively soft, being wood and should not scratch your paintwork. I saw a wonderful example of absolutely filthy parcels stock parked in a siding in Plymouth. Some wag had fingered 'Also available in blue' into its grimy surface.

So far we have dealt with rolling stock in somewhat general terms since I felt that taking you through the processes in a basic format would at least allow you to become familiar with the equipment and terminology used. You will no doubt discover which of the procedures suit your skills and will probably adopt other ways which may prove either simpler or more effective than those already discussed. That's part of the fun. So, now I'll take you through the step by step procedure for weathering a specific model or two.

A 7mm offering from RJH built by Geoff Grayson. I've painted the bodywork BR maroon using cellulose and the lining is in enamel paint – my first attempt using the Bob Moore Lining Pen as advertised in the model press. I've not got it quite right yet, but perseverance will no doubt reap its own rewards. Airbrushed with my usual weathering mix which is then removed using enamel thinners as described in the text and the residue remains trapped in the nooks and crannies.

GOODS WAGONS
BR STANDARD 16 TON MINERAL WAGON

Freight stock can be readily seen in a variety of finishes, even today with the wonderful assortment of liveries that BR seems destined to change almost every other week. The open steel mineral wagon has, in varying forms, been around since the 'forties and, whilst those modelling earlier periods will not therefore have a use for them, there is a large body of railway constructors out there who would be able to justify at least one or two of these ubiquitous wagons on any post-war layout depicting any region in the country. The weathering procedures which follow could also be applied to other steel wagons such as hoppers or even lineside structures, whether a bridge, water tower or just a basic oil drum.

For practical purposes, it is easier to illustrate the effects by selecting a 7 mm scale model and therefore I have chosen the ABS white metal and brass kit as our example. The methods are also suitable for smaller scales but these require even more delicate and subtle touches to produce the desired realism without overstating the abuse of the wagon concerned. Sometimes I rue the day I moved up to 7 mm because the models are much easier to scrutinise in close detail and if it's there on the real thing, you really have no option but to show it on the model. I suspect that this is one of the main reasons for going 7 mm in the first place since it provides just that extra challenge to produce convincing models.

An advantage of working with models based upon more recent times is the tremendous choice of excellent colour photographs available from which you can select the most suitable examples for your weathering projects. Books and magazines have any number of colour shots showing these wagons in all their shabby glory and I have chosen one which indicates the vehicle is badly in need of some loving care and attention.

One of my earlier attempts at weathering a steel mineral wagon ended up looking more like a military camouflage wagon because I created the patches of rust almost at random without paying attention to my own motto of painting what I saw rather than what I imagined it might have looked like. A case of 'Do what I say, not what I do', I'm afraid. If you think about it logically, the

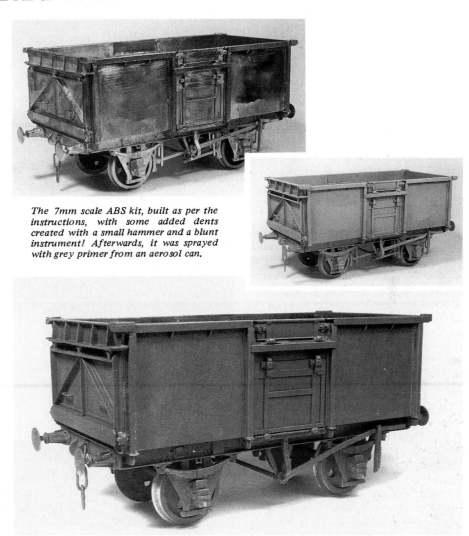

The 7mm scale ABS kit, built as per the instructions, with some added dents created with a small hammer and a blunt instrument! Afterwards, it was sprayed with grey primer from an aerosol can.

With the underframe sprayed cellulose black from a can and 'rust' stippled over the entire body, this second wagon is ready for the next stage.

rusted areas are formed in quite obvious places, frequently due to the paintwork being clouted or worn away as a result of loading and unloading, or simply through time expiry of the paint itself. As with anything else, the paint usually wears pretty thin on all sharp edges and once the elements have got to work and water has seeped under the paint, it can start to rust the metal exposed beneath. This eventually causes larger chunks of paint to peel or flake away from the rust bubbling up underneath and so the process continues until most of the paint has disappeared or the paintshops get hold of it to halt the process.

Assuming the model has been constructed as per the instructions and any extra detail required has been added, the basic priming procedures should be followed as already described and the model set aside to dry and harden off. This is probably one of those occasions when it doesn't matter whether you choose grey or red oxide primer since the top coat of BR Grey or Bauxite will not be much bothered by either shade if you decide to give the poor old wagon the full decrepit treatment. Were we selecting an almost ex-works or perhaps just recently overhauled finish, then we should be better advised to match the primer with the intended top coat colour.

Having primed the model, the underframe should be sprayed either from a car aerosol can in matt black or from your airbrush using cellulose. This is only to provide a tough finish to the paint prior to wellying in with the gunk and grot. Should any of the weathering wear away for any reason, then only a dark matt black colour will be revealed which shouldn't notice to the casual observer.

The entire body should be treated to a coating of rust including the interior. The build up of rust can be much more severe on a mineral wagon through total lack of maintenance, so don't be afraid to splodge in oodles of the talc with your orange/bauxite/black paint, giving a really heavily corroded appearance. If you use a stippling action, i.e. short vertical stabs with the brush, this will create a much more textured effect, producing a speckled finish. The chassis can now be treated in a similar manner, blending in the various colours as we described in the earlier section dealing with steam locomotive underframes.

If you have another project to work on, this would be a good time to get on with it, because you should put the mineral wagon aside for several hours to dry and harden off. Do not be tempted to go into the next stage any earlier because the processes which follow will ruin all your efforts so far if you haven't allowed sufficient drying time.

Working closely with your chosen photographs of the genuine article, use Humbrol Maskol to cover all those areas of the body where you want rust to show through. This part of the process is most vital in creating the realistic appearance we require, so it shouldn't be rushed. It is fairly tedious, but you must take your time and place the tiniest spots of the Maskol where you want only the smallest of rust patches to show. Some rusting effects will be added after the wagon is almost completed, so, if you think there are some nooks and crannies where it will be difficult to retrieve the Maskol with the tweezers, ignore those parts until later. The rubbery solution dries and solidifies fairly swiftly so you can start mixing your topcoat colour ready for brushing on when the Maskol has set.

In this example, we have selected a BR Grey livery suitable for unfitted wagons and I would recommend using enamel paint (I use Railmatch) – in fact cellulose would probably be useless for this particular weathering procedure as it would dry too hard and possibly be detrimental to the 'rust' already painted on. The paint should be hand brushed on rather than airbrushed

Maskol applied as per the text and, once dry, the body is brush-painted using Railmatch BR Grey.

since we want to apply a fairly thick single coat in order for the paint to flake and chip realistically. This should now be set aside to dry. If you have to go out for a few hours or do something else, then all well and good – it saves you from getting impatient and starting the next stage too early.

I know I do go on a bit about this, but weathering cannot be rushed. I have seen several efforts brought to me by modellers who say they don't know what all the fuss is about when it comes to weathering. They then proudly thrust their latest creations in front of me and say it took just half an hour to produce. Unfortunately, this is only too obvious. As far as I am concerned, there are no short cuts to producing a realistic model. Here endeth the lecture . . .

Returning to your wagon, you will observe a most dreadful paint finish with lumps and bumps all over the shop. Don't panic, that's how it's supposed to look. We now come to the most interesting part of the procedure. Take a pair of tweezers and gently pluck the bits of Maskol from the wagon body. If you've allowed the paint to dry sufficiently, the Maskol will come away, leaving the rust exposed underneath and the topcoat grey paint will flake around the edges in a most realistic manner. If you applied the Maskol in multitudes of tiny patches, it should take some while to retrieve all of the bits and you may find that gently rubbing your finger over the lumps will cause them to come away quite easily. Be careful, otherwise you will remove all of the flaking paint if you are too heavy fingered. The end result is a wagon which has flaking and peeling paint almost everywhere.

That was the most exciting part, and we now need to bring the damage to life by highlighting all of the flakes of plaint plus the rust underneath. Look closely at your photograph and you will see that the flaked paint edges have further signs of rust at their outer limits and orange/brown stains run in faint streaks downwards from the lower edges. The model doesn't quite capture that effect yet, so we shall need to simulate those stains by very carefully drybrushing the flaked edges first with Bauxite/Orange and then slightly less so with Gunmetal. The paint flakes should now have very old rust at their outer limits, fading into the orangey stains of new rusting activity.

The larger rust patches, which at the moment are looking a little flat and uninteresting, will also need highlighting. If the patches are dark in colour, drybrush gently across them with a lighter Orange/Bauxite mix. The dried paint/talcum powder should be quite textured and will have lots of tiny gritty bits which will highlight very easily. The brush to use is a soft 'flattie' with the barest hint of paint still attached. The reason for originally coating the entire body in the 'rust' mix will now become evident because the areas which weren't protected by the Maskol will be grey painted but still having a slightly textured surface to them. Once again using the Gunmetal/Orange blend, very delicately drybrush the surface of the painted areas and you will see lots of tiny specks suddenly appearing as though fresh rusting activity is still taking place underneath the topcoat of paint. At the same time stipple the Gunmetal/Orange

After the paint has thoroughly dried, the Maskol is plucked from the bodywork with a pair of tweezers.

With the Maskol removed, the 'rust' beneath is revealed surrounded by flaking paint.

Black numbering patches are applied, and some drybrushing and general abuse, by scuffing and scratching, etc., has begun.

Lettering and numbering completed and protected with acrylic varnish. The off-white line and chalk inscriptions are in place and, after a final toning down from the airbrush, she's ready to earn her keep.

into those nooks and crannies you earlier opted to leave until later. If gently done, the stippled areas will create softer edges to the rusty patches in contrast to the more striking flaked parts.

You should begin to see the wagon looking fairly convincingly like the photographs and you can now paint in the matt blue/black patches where the lettering and numbering will go. Leave the bodywork to dry and if you can avoid handling it the underframe may be highlighted, drybrushing the axleboxes and springs etc. Once the paint is touch dry, a dusting with talcum powder using a clean, dry paintbrush will add further sparkling highlights to selected areas. Paint the brake lever end cream/white and, when dry, gently drybrush with gunmetal or gunmetal/orange to show wear and tear. As previously mentioned, Grey/Metalcote Gunmetal used sparingly simulates a blue oily effect over axleboxes and any areas where oil may have gathered. I should emphasise that the Metalcote Gunmetal should not be confused with the standard Gunmetal (53) which is not really suitable for this effect. If you're still with me and haven't dozed off from fatigue or just plain boredom, we are nearing the end at last.

The three-link couplings should be chemically blackened rather than painted, if using Slaters' links which I find to be most accurate in proportions. They are a bright steel but, after dunking in the Perma-Blue or Carr's blackening fluids (any one of their range seems to work), they will dry to a realistic used steel appearance and will remain so with no fear of paint coming off, exposing the bright metal again. You will need to neutralise the blackening fluids by rinsing in water otherwise the chemical process will continue unabated and the links will actually chemically begin to rust. Aha! – useful, you may be thinking, but the rusting process will eventually clog the links making them difficult to couple up to an adjacent wagon. I know, there's no pleasing some folk.

Back to the bodywork and we can now paint in the off-white stripe which denotes the end doors. I'm not particularly good at painting straight white lines so I usually press a strip of sellotape onto the side, cut out the stripe area using a scalpel and steel rule, then paint in the white stripe by brush. It doesn't really matter if some paint seeps under the tape edges, it adds to the effect, although if you really don't like it you can stipple rust over the offending bits later. It would be wise to reduce the tackiness of the tape by first of all repeatedly pressing it onto any clean, flat surface and pulling it off again. If it is too sticky, you run the risk of the paint and the 'rust' beneath coming away with the tape when you peel it off. Alternatively, the white line area is lightly scored into the paintwork with a scalpel and you paint the stripe freehand with the score lines acting as natural boundaries. The lines themselves won't show if you don't score them too deeply. Stippling rust along the outer edge of the scoreline will disguise it anyway.

After you have lettered and numbered the wagon on the black patches, protect the transfers with matt acrylic varnish brushed on, and again leave to dry. We're nearly there now.

You may find some wagons have quite heavy scratch marks and gouges in the sides and these are simulated in a number of ways. For the heavier marks, you literally take a scalpel or a blunt needle and scar the paintwork, after which you can paint in the gouges with Metalcote Gunmetal if the marks are supposedly recent or with Gunmetal/Bauxite/Orange if a little older. Also, take fairly coarse sandpaper and gently sand the surface of the paint in various different directions. This will add dozens of fine blemishes to the painted finish, adding even more texture to the model. The interior of the wagon could probably do

with a bit of abuse since it usually gets bashed and scratched more frequently by the items carried within it. Again, various abrasive treatments can be inflicted upon it, given that the interiors, as far as I am aware, were never painted at all and would rot away happily ad infinitum.

Now put the model aside to completely dry for several hours because we are about to come to the final stage.

Some articles in magazines have indicated how the writer 'weathered' his model

by sploshing dirty turps all over it and leaving it at that. You will by now have gathered that this is not quite how it's done, but we are about to do something very similar to our wagon, although it is only at this point in our weathering processes where I will recommend so doing.

Gently apply a wash of enamel thinners over the entire wagon body and whilst wet, touch neat matt Gunmetal/Bauxite to the surface. This will cause the dark colours to be drawn into all of the hollows and crevices

The first wagon has not been subjected to the Maskol treatment — instead I wanted a softer effect and proceeded with the remainder of the treatments as before. Rust patches were gently stippled on over the topcoat.

The other side of the wagon featured on the previous page, showing less signs of stress.

A third vehicle weathered employing a combination of all of the methods used on the other two wagons.

by capillary action which will add depth to the textured surfaces. It will create artificial shadows around the raised bits which will have the knock-on effect of highlighting those same raised parts. Similarly, you can touch the wet surfaces around rivets and bolts with Yellow/Orange which will leave tiny rings of fresh 'rust' surrounding the raised detail.

For further subtle variations in the textured finish, a delicate blending in of some weathering powders would probably add character to the overall finish if you feel that certain something is lacking. It's difficult to advise you here because only your own experimentation with the various processes we have discussed will decide which methods give you the results you seek. I'm all for wellying in with everything I can find in order to provide the quite complex variety of textures and colour tones evident on the prototype. I often spend hours fussing over just one wagon side until I'm happy with the end result, but not everyone has the time or possibly the inclination to go to such lengths.

When all is dry, add the last touch of realism, which is the scribbled chalk messages usually to be found on any wagon. These could be notes on the condition of the wagon, its destination or simply markings made to show the shunter which wagon is to be placed in what order, etc. I have used a white chinagraph pencil sharpened to a very fine point to some effect and this is available from any art shop of even W. H. Smiths. Also a simple writing pen of the old pen and inkwell school variety can be used with white Indian ink, which are also available from the same sources.

You should now be able to place the model on your layout, stand back and admire a respectable representation of the real thing. You will note that the airbrush has not been used at all so far, unless you used it initially to prepare the underframe, but it certainly isn't crucial to the above procedures. Now would be the only time I might just spray a very light brownish dusting over the wagon to tone down or 'yellow off' the lettering and stripe if necessary. You will now have probably become sick of the sight of mineral wagons so you should place the model in a box and tuck it away somewhere safe for a few days. Then retrieve it and see if it still looks right to you. If it does – it probably is.

PLANKED WAGONS

Probably more common throughout railway history are the open wooden planked wagons plus box vans which therefore require a section to themselves.

Consideration must be given to exactly how the wagon should be portrayed. No vehicle is ever alike – neither then should your models appear the same. Some wagons could be in pristine condition (almost ex-works), others could be quite well painted with the odd plank showing signs of wear and tear, or at the other extreme, some could have no paintwork at all, with just patches painted on to enable identifying information to stand out clearly.

In earlier times, private owner wagons were kept fairly smart whilst in latter years, they might still be running long after the original owners had faded into obscurity, and thus the painted names and ancillary lettering or numbering may also have faded in similar manner. Really you need to research thoroughly your chosen subject and select a good photograph to work from.

Let's begin with an open wagon which is in fair condition but which is showing definite signs of wear. The basic preparatory work naturally will depend upon the type of materials from which your wagon is constructed – if a metal kit it will require priming as discussed in earlier chapters, but if a plastic kit or proprietary item, you can start the basic treatment immediately. The underframe should be dealt with first – you will perhaps have developed your techniques sufficiently for it to become relatively straightforward by now and the amount of weathering to be utilised should be self evident if you refer to your photographs.

For the bodywork, it is my advice to start with the interior because you can handle the exterior without fear of marking paintwork since you haven't applied it yet!

Many model open wagons are seen featured on layouts where the builder has painted the inside the same livery as the outside. I'm pretty certain the interiors of wagons were never painted at all (no doubt someone will cite an example to prove me wrong) because there was simply no need to. The image of the railway companies was perpetuated by the exterior paintwork not the interior. It is sometimes quite tricky finding suitable photographic evidence to show how the inside of a wagon actually looked. Most pictures are taken from one

The first picture shows a typical open wagon whose lettering and numbers (in 1938) look more recent than the paintwork, whereas the second (photographed in 1950) is just showing its earlier insignia plus later (but already out-of-date) numbering and lettering. A new plank and a chalk inscription add atmosphere.
WESSEX COLLECTION

side or three-quarters on so that the interior is hidden either because of the angle of shot, or maybe because the wagon has a full load which obscures the view. Do not despair. If you are able to take some of your own photographs of wagons from your local goods yard or preserved line, all well and good, but an alternative is to visit perhaps your local builders yard where open lorries come and go all day. Seek permission to take shots of the interiors of these when the tail gates are let down and you will have the identical colours and weathering which can be found inside any railway truck. Similarly, when sitting in the dreaded traffic queues on your way to or from town, rather than mutter to yourself when stuck behind the old weatherbeaten lorry, notice the way its planked end is scratched and damaged through years of use and how the securing chains and bolts have rusted and then stained the woodwork. I don't suggest you leap out and gleefully take photographs, but instead make mental notes for future reference. As I said at the beginning of the book, there are few items around us which don't bear some signs of weathering and they don't have to be railway related to show how man and nature leave their marks upon the world, so observe and inwardly digest all the time until it becomes a habit.

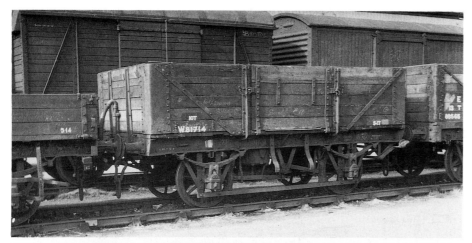

Two examples of wagons, probably unpainted but possibly with bauxite patches on the first (as it's vacuum fitted) to give a cleaner background for the lettering and numbers. Daylight can be seen peeping between the planks. The second is most likely adorned with black painted patches which are more usual on unfitted vehicles.   ROYE ENGLAND

Generally speaking, timberwork inside a wagon gets pretty scruffy fairly swiftly and rather than paint it one colour such as 'Natural Wood' from the enamel paint range, study the colours for yourself and the wood will probably appear as an almost indefinable beige/grey with lots of lines and grooves showing up darker where the wood grain and knots are. This, plus all the dents, scratches and rust streaks from the strapping and securing bolts, will add extra subtle colours, creating a fine assortment of murky hues. Where do you begin?

Well, first brush paint the interior sides and floor with matt enamel light grey (64) and 'natural wood' (110) or 'dark earth' (29) plus a little matt black (33) at random, blending them all together whilst still wet. Don't worry about avoiding the 'metal-work' because that can be picked out later. Make sure the whole of the interior gets a fairly healthy covering and then leave to dry completely because the next stage is to drybrush each plank with lighter and darker shades of these colours using a flat brush and only in the direction of the 'grain'. Gunmetal (53) is ideal for representing well-worn woodwork when drybrushed on (and is particularly useful for telegraph poles, etc, creating a fairly convincing representation of weathered creosote). However, when mixed with other greys, it sometimes takes on a rather green tint, so unless that is what you require, be careful. Keep this going until you are happy with it and then leave to dry again.

The nearest open has cracks, knots and gouges from long service. Note the steel strapping along the top edges (half-round beading would probably fit the bill). The strapping and bolts rust away merrily and this in turn stains the nearby timber.

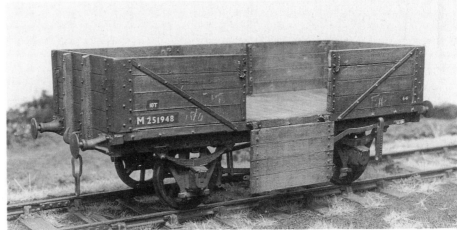

My own interpretation using an ABS 7mm wagon treated as described in the text.

Top to bottom: beige/grey paint followed by horizontal drybrushing going with the 'grain', then vertical treatment plus abrasions and scratches using emery paper. Finally, once dry, the dark diluted thinners lends some depth to the grooves and indentations.

The next stage is to drybrush across the planks in the opposite direction to the grain, using up and down or vertical movements to show staining and scratches, following the laws of gravity. This should be very subtly done; better to understate than overstate the effects or they will look too contrived and ruin the whole thing. Now comes the vandalism. When the paint had totally dried and hardened, take small pieces of fine to medium emery paper and gently abrade the painted surfaces in both horizontal and vertical directions to texturise the paint surface and create genuine grain ridges and furrows. At the same time, randomly rub the emery paper across the planks in various different directions rather like a scrubbing action, which will create hundreds of simulated scratches and dents to indicate the multitude of tiny blemishes caused by the various loads over the years.

If you are dealing with a white metal kit and the scratching plus abrading process goes through the paint and exposes white metal underneath, panic ye not for it will respond well to the old liquid Gun Blue or Carr's blackening agents. Simply dip a cotton bud into your selected chemical and rub the white metal with it and it should darken to a dull sheen, whereupon a further drybrushing with suitable colours followed

This 7mm scale ABS fitted BR 5-plank open has corrugated ends which permits some variety in weathering techniques to be employed.

Some of the bauxite paint is just starting to bubble up.

by the emery paper should restore all to its former glory again. This blackening process is useful for exposed edges of whitemetal kits of all sorts. Paint wears away from these edges due to frequent handling and the exposed areas can be left blackened without need of further painting if you wish. These chemicals don't take too well on etched brass other than producing light patchy staining which rubs off after a while, so sharp edges can be coated in a thin smear of superglue which are then painted once dried into a hardened film.

Now the metalwork is picked out in a mix of Gunmetal (53), Bauxite (133) and Grey (64) which should achieve a fairly well-worn rusty steel appearance, and again this should be left to dry completely because there then follows the 'sploshing on the enamel thinners' bit, and it is vital that all paintwork is completely dry and hardened otherwise your thinners will wash away all of your handiwork to date! So gently apply the thinners and, whilst wet, add in a little Matt Black/Bauxite so that the dirty thinners will be drawn into all of

A different angle and the left-hand lettering is transferred straight onto the bauxite paintwork which was the normal practice, whilst the right-hand end's tare weight is more unusually printed onto a black patch. A little variety does no harm and it's quite prototypical.

the grooves and scratches. The metalwork can have fresh rust stains indicated by the same process as used on earlier subjects, i.e. touching the raised detail with tiny droplets of neat Orange/Leather which, when the thinners have evaporated, will leave miniscule stains surrounding the boltheads and where the metalwork meets the woodwork. For added effect, taking a fine brush, very delicate rust stains may be streaked downwards from the base of the strapping or individual bolts either whilst the thinners are still wet or afterwards when everything has dried out. Try not to rush this stage — take your time and do small areas at a go, and re-wet the surface again if you feel so inclined. Put the wagon away somewhere and later come back to it to see afresh how it looks.

You may wish to add further stress marks or scratches and perhaps more highlights to the planks and strapping with extra drybrushing. The processes can be carried on until you are happy with the result. A last gentle brushing over the interior with talc will both tone down some areas and add a subtle sparkle to others.

For wagons which are mostly unpainted or which perhaps have had planks replaced without painting, all and any of the above procedures may be adopted for the exterior planking. For those planks which have been painted but which are now showing signs of blistered paintwork, they should first be treated as the interior and then you may try gently polishing the paint until a hardened sheen appears, either by using a mop in your electric modelling drill, or just by fairly vigorous rubbing with a cloth. Now brush paint the planks, leaving maybe the odd tiny area unpainted, although this is

Another close-up draws attention to the texture of the rusted corner plate and strapping plus the cracked and scarred planks. Lighter fresh rust rings are forming about the top strapping retaining clips. Spend a long time just studying photographs of the prototype, absorbing as much information as possible. I think it pays dividends.

Drybrushing the metalwork with assorted grimy colours, plus the oil streaks on the axlebox, afterwards adding rust rings around the bolt-heads, will provide further illusions of wear and tear.

not vital, and leave to dry completely. Using Day-Wat Liquid Poly, lightly dab some of the topcoat paintwork with a brush and you will see it start to craze and bubble. Don't touch it at all until several hours later, because the paint must be allowed to harden again before the next stage in the treatment.

There are a number of choices now:

1. You may lightly scrape across the surface of the bubbled paint with a flat screwdriver blade so that small flakes of paint are chipped away.
2. Gently scrub the paintwork with the emery paper which will have a similar effect to the above but with finer flakes being removed.
3. Use a fibreglass pencil to do all of the above and also to fade the remaining paintwork, creating a more worn effect.
4. Leave the paintwork as it is in its crazed condition, then gently drybrush across the raised surface of the crazed paint using lighter shades of the main body topcoat colour, which will highlight the edges and indicate the paintwork is losing its colour at those highlighted points.

You can combine any or all of the above – it's up to you. The reason for initially polishing and thus hardening the 'wooden'

Another 7mm scale ABS fitted wagon in bauxite, treated as per the text, plus an interior shot of the unfitted open with all its scratches and general abuse.

7mm scale ABS unfitted open with attendant insignia and chalk scribblings. The tarpaulin (made from masking tape) was weathered by drybrushing plus some additional painted-in shadows and highlights to give the illusion of creases — particularly where the ropes tug at their securing points. Some of the creases are, of course, real. Can you tell them apart?

Interior of a 7-plank open shows the rough treatment the wood received in everyday use.

The same wagon's exterior. Note the buckled top strapping, the opening door which has dropped slightly, breaking up the horizontal plank symmetry, and the painted door end strip which is slowly being pushed away from the steel strapping by the rust beneath. The 'P' prefix denotes its private owner origins.

areas was to ensure that the Day-Wat bubbled only the topcoat of paint and didn't remove your hard work underneath. (The polished areas will become less shiny again during the above processes.)

To create much larger patches of flaking or peeling paintwork, you will need to follow the procedures we discussed for the steel mineral wagon, using Maskol to protect the woodwork. Certainly the strapping and cornerplates can be treated this way since it will be similar in appearance to the steel wagon. For more subtle rusting of the metalwork, simple stippling of your favourite 'rust' mix onto the topcoat will suffice. Highlight the top edge strapping on the wagon sides and ends by painting in Gunmetal to indicate polished use, and even if your wagon doesn't have this strapping modelled, painting the top edges will create the illusion it's there.

Now patches for lettering should be painted on or just simple application of company logos, after which they could either be protected with an acrylic matt varnish (preferably by airbrush) or the lettering can be abraded with emery paper, fibreglass pencil or fine scalpel blade. This should effectively create a much more worn and haggard look to the lettering.

Say, for example, you have initially lettered your wagon in private owner or just pre-grouping corporate insignia, you could treat this to a fair amount of abuse until it has almost completely disappeared. If you now varnish the entire area with acrylic matt varnish and then apply fresh insignia of a later period, you can gently weather that down to a more used appearance. A final dusting with talc will complete the process, or perhaps just a light toning down from the airbrush to mellow the colours and the brightness of the lettering. Hopefully, the end result will be a convincing model of a well-worn wagon whose original ownership can just barely be made out appearing underneath the latter owner's insignia.

A short cut would be to use a pre-printed private owner wagon such as that made by Slaters and distress the lettering before application of the next processes. For a faded effect I have found gentle vertical streaking with a cotton bud *dampened* with Day-Wat Liquid Poly will slowly melt the lettering and cause the pigments to run quite realistically. Be careful here because too drastic treatment will cause the lettering to melt away completely and take on the appearance of a water colour painting

This example still bears remnants of its original ownership but general wear and tear plus replacement planks here and there are slowly obscuring its history. ROYE ENGLAND

An 'after and before' photo of a Slater's pre-printed 7mm wagon side. The procedures are detailed in the text.

A close-up showing the assortment of textures and effects.

which has been rained upon. Not very realistic!

If you don't want to risk the Day-Wat, you might try simply rubbing the lettering in downward (top to bottom) actions with a fibreglass brush. This will eventually fade the lettering, but be wary of too vigorous use because the lettering will scratch and this may not be the effect you seek.

For wagons with less worn paintwork, either drybrush the topcoat with slightly lighter shades of the colour used or blend in lighter and darker shades whilst the topcoat is still wet during the initial painting, just to create delicate variations in the body colour. Then proceed as above for the lettering etc. An overall wash with dirty thinners will trap darker colours in the joints between the planks to create further contrast.

If you're really careful with a very fine scalpel blade, you can cut right through the joints so that daylight can just be seen between them. Carve the edges as if some of the woodwork has worn away and the whole wagon will appear that little bit more ramshackle. Don't overdo it though, unless you intend having it parked in a siding with a condemned sign attached. It should still look as though it's capable of carrying a reasonable weight without fear of collapse. Don't forget the chalk scribblings of the shunter or warehouseman to add that extra realism.

Two similar vehicles which offer much valuable visual information to the observant. The first appears to have its original planking still intact while the second has had one new plank on the left-hand side at some time, and, more recently, completely new door timbers onto which are painted the two short white lines which show it is fitted with bottom opening doors in its floor. The photographer chalked in the remains of this wagon's original number for reference purposes.
ROYE ENGLAND

A final shot in this section illustrates an ex-NE wagon — betrayed by the last vestiges of the 'E' adorning three of the six original planks surviving on this side. The remainder appear quite recent and obviously unpainted. Many wagons remained so until final scrapping. Look at the patterns and knots of the fresher timber, the top strapping lifting here and there, plus its retaining clips — all but one out of true. Just visible is the last evidence of the original corner-to-corner stripe which signified the end door, now indicated by the faded white stripe on the right-hand side strapping. What a challenge to reproduce this one!

Van roof planks often showed through the canvas, as seen in this view taken at Weymouth.   NATIONAL RAILWAY MUSEUM

BOX VANS

For the standard box van, with the exception of the interior (unless it is shown with doors open) the above ground rules apply. The roof should be treated in much the same way as your coaches, although if you really want to go to town on it (figuratively speaking), you may want to try the following.

The canvas used on the roofs of vans does deteriorate with time and certain patches finally split and peel back, exposing bare planks beneath. To portray this damage, first study photographs in order to see on which parts of van roofs these most commonly occur. Then using a scraperboard blade, scribe in small areas of planking (you will need to press harder on metal roofs) and indicate where the nailheads appear by prodding a couple of indentations at each plank end with a compass point. Use emery paper to sand off any raised burrs and run a scalpel blade down the plank grooves to deepen the joins. Now paint these 'planks'

The pale areas of the lower planks on this GW van show evidence of continual chalking and rubbing out of destinations, etc. The residue of chalk dust has become ingrained in the timber.
ROYE ENGLAND

A 7mm scale Freightman van routinely weathered but with the roof peeling as described in the text.

in exactly the same way as you produced the open wagon interiors by drybrushing with Gunmetal (53) and 'Natural wood' (110) until a grained appearance results. When this has dried, protect these patches with Maskol and after this has dried, paint the entire roof with a mixture of Tarmac (No. 112) and talcum powder, giving it plenty of texture and wait for this to dry completely.

Taking a pair of tweezers, gently pluck the Maskol from the roof and with a bit of luck, the 'planks' will be exposed with the roof 'canvas' flaking and peeling at the edges. Other parts of the roof can be flooded with Day-Wat Liquid Poly which should cause a rippling effect in the paint, which could be taken for creases in the canvas. Another way to represent these creases is to apply Tippex typing correction fluid in thin wavy lines on various parts of the roof. The Tippex dries quickly and if you repeatedly build up more layers in the same places, when the paint/talc mix is subsequently applied, the ripples under the surface with look quite convincing.

Now the entire roof can be gently washed with the dirty thinners mixture so

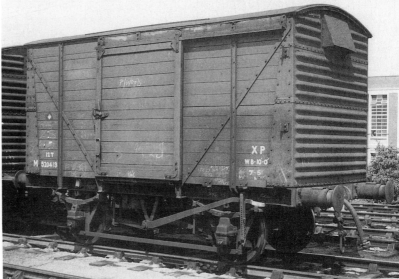

This van has fairly subtle changes in paint shades, decorated with a multitude of chalked inscriptions indicating the contents of the van, its destinations, dates of inspection, etc.

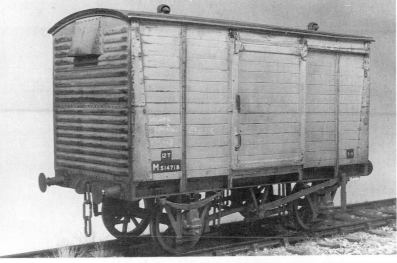

A Freightman unfitted van whose sides are lightly weathered. This time I have drawn attention to the corrugated ends which are showing more serious signs of wear and have drybrushed them using Metalcote Gunmetal and Bauxite using a flattie brush.

This SR 12-ton vehicle has very distinctive roof strips and the canvas has wrinkles and creases. These can either be painted on to create the illusion they are there — much as with the tarpaulin sheet earlier — or very fine applications of Tippex correction fluid from a thin brush would be better, before spraying with your selected roof colour. **WESSEX COLLECTION**

An end view with the specially painted panel for the shunters' comments. Don't forget the polished or oily buffer heads on your stock which are easily represented either using a lead pencil or by touching in with a paint brush dipped in an oil rust mix. Barely discernible are some stencilled-in notes at the top centre of the wagon. **WESSEX COLLECTION**

that the grain of the wood, joints and the nail heads will trap the dirt and bring them to life. A weathering spray from the airbrush with light variations of your by now well-established general filth mixture will indicate the wagon has been running in this condition for some time. I suggest you only take this amount of trouble on one or two wagon roofs or it will appear overly done. Sometimes it is the simple touch which creates character in your models such as the fairly well weatherbeaten box van which has had one door replaced which has already been painted in ex-works finish prior to fitting. It stands out quite distinctly amongst the other stock and its prototype can be found in many photographs to prove the point.

As on the prototype, at some stage new wagons issued forth from the paintshops and one or two in almost ex-works condition should look quite acceptable on your layout. Even so, they would almost immediately show at least some signs of initial weathering and I suggest you would be wise to represent them likewise. If you don't, the wagons could look too much like models and we don't want that, do we?

A close-up of my 7mm model of a fitted van built from another Freightman kit — lots of texture to give the timber character.

Two views of the same van bearing a few chalk marks and the remains of a sticker (Tippex correction fluid) just to add a little contrast.

A batch of WR vans in various states of repair, each with its own characteristic features. Remember that no two vehicles are ever totally alike and there is often the temptation to have one of each type of wagon on your layout, either to avoid unnecessary repetition or simply because you want your pick-up goods to appear interesting. Weather identical types of vehicles in totally different states of repair and you will achieve the same result when mixed in with other stock similarly treated. It was rare to see a freight train containing no 'repeats' in its make-up.

ROYE ENGLAND

Another 7mm scale model — an ABS fruit van in reasonable order, although most of the planks are showing early signs of wear.

An ex-LNER offering from the same stable and this van's woodwork is just a little more distressed than that of the fruit van. Liquid Poly to bubble the top coat, followed by much scraping and sanding, should produce similar results on your own stock.

Ex-LNER Brake Van from a 7mm scale Slater's kit, with steel platforms rather than the concrete items fitted to the later BR versions.

The paint is bubbling and splitting on the ducket, exposing rusting metal beneath, while the planking is bearing signs of multiple abrasions.

7mm scale 'U' Class 2—6—0 No. 31794 about to leave Hursley with its brake van.

This sequence shows a Lima 4mm UKF wagon as purchased, then sprayed with an even coating of grime, and the weathering partly removed exactly as described in the diesel loco section, leaving stained and ingrained paintwork. Extra hard rubbing with the cotton bud and thinners will fade the lettering realistically.

A reasonably clean tank wagon with just faint streaks of dirt running from top to bottom.

A little more grime on this one, plus some spots and scratches.

Petrol tanks being discharged at Swindon Town in 1952.

ROYE ENGLAND

TANK WAGONS

One item which does create its own peculiar difficulties from the weathering point of view is the simple tank wagon. Due to its unique shape, the effects of spillage and subsequent staining are quite distinctive and also very logical when you think about it. Gravitational forces dictate that usually the dribbles and build-up of goo run vertically – seldom horizontally. In general traffic use, these tanks can get pretty grimy and although cleaned from time to time, are rarely seen in ex-works condition. Under private ownership at industrial premises, they can frequently be seen in a dreadful state, defying most attempts at identifying who the owner is, let alone what's being transported.

In this next exercise, we shall run through the procedures for producing a well-weathered tank wagon which has partly been cleaned before a further build-up of grime has again started to adhere.

The order of play is quite straightforward. First of all establish that the chosen model, if a commercially produced ready-to-run item, has had its painting and lettering printed or painted on and then transfers added afterwards. Some thinners will remove the manufactured finish if you're not careful, and, whilst this can be useful

for certain effects, it can be fairly drastic if all the lettering suddenly disappears in one go! Check by using a cotton bud dipped in enamel thinners on some part of the wagon whose final appearance may be obscured at a later stage. If the paint or transfers start to come away, then you will need to spray the entire wagon with a fine coating of

protective acrylic varnish. If your own kit-built tank, then you will be able to decide how best to apply your paint and transfers according to the end result you seek.

In this particular example, it would be better to use a satin acrylic varnish, firstly because we don't require a matt finish to show through the weathering and secondly

The lettering was possibly applied without first re-painting this vehicle since it appears in better condition than the metalwork beneath.

A Hornby Shell Oils wagon after receiving its first signs of spillage, courtesy of the airbrush.

Other coatings have been applied and now removed as per the text.

The wagon could remain in its semi-cleaned state, but I have added a dusting of traffic grime to subdue the overall finish.

Fresh spillage is again sprayed from filler to base line.

because the later processes will use enamel thinners which would, if not careful, remove an enamel-based varnish as well as the weathering. Once again, it's vital to study a photograph or three before commencing work. Remember we must reproduce what we see, not what we think we see. Don't try to imagine how the weathering stains appear, look at the real thing and copy that – it's much simpler.

The prototype chosen is an oil tank wagon as this creates stains of greater contrast from an illustrative point of view. First of all mix up an oily colouring using Metalcote Gunmetal with a little matt grey (No. 64), and gently spray the top of the wagon in and around the fillers and run the airbrush in short downward strokes, starting above the wagon (remember the section on airbrushing), moving down past the fillers and fanning out towards the middle or waist of the tank (finger eased back off the throttle here) and then increasing the plaint flow and slightly increasing the airflow as the paint reaches the lower part of the tank. In other words, we are trying to show that the oil spillage builds up more densely on the lower regions of the tank whilst it is less able to cling to the waist area as this is almost vertical. As it gloops down past the waistline, it is able to cling once more to the underside of the tank, being trapped amongst the brake dust and general grime which has sprayed up from the wheels in service.

What also happens is that the build-up in the lower regions causes the subsequent deposits to fan out somewhat and be drawn along the base line by capillary action where the tank is joined to the chassis. We must attempt to copy this effect by arcing the airbrush in a flaring action to right and left of the central area. Study photographs if you're not sure what I'm getting at. Once content that this all looks correct, the tank wagon can now be given a general weathering from the airbrush using your favourite traffic grime mix. I favour Metalcote Gunmetal with Leather (No. 62) increasing the Leather content in subsequent oversprayings to show brake dust build-up. Again, the waistline appears to be less covered in most photographs and you simply continue until the vehicle looks pretty murky. You can, if you wish, repeat the first stage, indicating fresh spillage over the traffic grime, it's up to you. Study your photographs and you will see that heavier spillage shows up just like paint runs, so we duplicate this appearance by loading the paintbrush with a blob of 'oil' and streaking it down the sides of the tank. You can then repeat the process again until you have several overlays of paint runs glooping down the sides of the tank.

If you now wish the wagon to remain in this uncleaned condition, simply drybrush the raised detail to bring it to life, and the reason for choosing Gunmetal in the oil mix will become clear. The mixture with the Grey, as we have previously mentioned, will lend a blue tint to the colour just as oil has this colour in its make-up, and gently polishing the oily areas with a finger tip or dry cotton bud will create an oily sheen. Taking a soft large brush and flicking it vertically back and forth over the tank sides will create tiny streaks in the build-up of weathering you have applied, which adds that little something to the overall appearance. Also, the action of gently polishing the sides will help stabilise the paint and reduce the risk of removal of your fine work by subsequent handling. You could varnish it, but, as I've said before, this flattens the

Dribbles of neat paint, allowed to run down the sides from a paintbrush, complete the sequence.

whole effect and takes away the shine and glitter of those subtle shades of colouring. However, some photographs indicate really shiny fresh spillage streaked down the sides and using gloss varnish over the oil stains will mimic this quite well.

Hopefully, the overall finish will please you and you may be inclined to leave it be, but our original intention was to show a tank wagon which has been subsequently partly cleaned, so we're going to undo a lot of what we've already done!

This six-wheel milk tank has dozens of tiny scratches or spillage lines which run almost in random directions. To reproduce this, once the spraying of the grime is completed, immediately run a reasonably stiff-haired bristle brush across the paint in similar directions and it should be feasible to mimic the original.
ROYE ENGLAND

It is just possible to make out the Esso lozenge logos under the dirt and spillage.   WESSEX COLLECTION

Photographed in 1957 at Weymouth, a Tarmac tank painted black somewhere under its sticky mantle. Blending talcum powder with a semi-gloss black paint or Metalcote Gunmetal would be one way of reproducing this sludgelike effect — dragging the brush hairs vertically over the mixture to simulate its rivulet patterns.

Slater's 7mm scale tank wagon kit which I've treated to a healthy dose of corrosion and sludge. I worked on the tank's effects before finally fixing in place to ensure continuity of flow down its sides uninterrupted by the support wires or end stanchions.

The next stage should be left until all of the applications of paint can harden off. Once the vehicle can be fairly roughly handled without any paint wearing away, it's probably ready.

Using enamel thinners and a cotton bud, gently rub the tank sides, moving from top to bottom in single strokes until the weathering starts to come adrift in streaks, exposing the paintwork beneath. Vary the pressure so that the streaks are almost totally random, and once you're happy that enough has been removed, stop. Now check with your photographs to ensure this looks quite authentic, and finally, if you wish, *lightly* spray the entire bodywork with the airbrush so that the streaks become somewhat toned down and faded beneath the coating. The overall result should indicate a partly cleaned tank which has subsequently resumed service and commenced a new build-up of grime.

If your tank wagon is intended to represent a vehicle transporting bitumen or tar, then you can further distress the surface of the oily areas by stippling in large quantities of talc when you apply the oily paint mix in the first place. Once this has hardened, a careful application of Day-Wat Liquid Poly to the oily patches will bubble the paint/talc mixture in the same way as we discovered earlier when painting coach roofs. This creates the appearance of melted tar and adds that extra bit of texture to your creation.

The modelled interior of Hursley locomotive shed with stained, whitewashed walls and concrete floor.

BUILDINGS

At the beginning, I suggested that model rolling stock can be much improved by some judicious wielding of the airbrush *et al*, but I also intimated that these efforts would appear far more convincing if its surroundings were similarly treated. In other words, there's little point in spending hours creating a masterpiece of artistic excellence if it's then plonked on a layout which doesn't match its status. So I think we'll have a cursory look at some buildings and other related items – specifically the representation and weathering of some of their constituent materials and see if it's possible to improve their appearance, adapting the techniques we've already covered.

BRICKWORK

It can be very tempting when modelling buildings to skimp over some of the more tedious parts because some structures are quite large – particularly in 7mm – and I certainly have to be in the right mood to carry out some of the more boring, repetitive procedures. When faced with acres of brickwork, it is easy to assume a brick is a brick, paint it brick red and get on with something else. Well, if you've gone to great lengths to establish the authenticity of your locomotives and other rolling stock, you really owe it to yourself to do the same for your buildings and scenery. The brickwork in your chosen area may not be red and could vary quite dramatically

from other parts of the country, so I would recommend you refer again to some colour photographs either of the particular building you have modelled or, if a freelance building, then at least one of a similar style and construction.

I have favoured rural Southern England locations in my modelling, therefore the examples illustrated are all from this part of the country. If your models are based elsewhere, it doesn't matter because the procedures don't change – only the choice of colours.

I've always used Slater's Plastikard for my structures, using their embossed brickwork for the outer finished walls, and the following procedures apply to this medium. If you use brickpapers, then the airbrush will permit some variation in effects but without the benefit of the raised detail which the plastikard enjoys. Similarly, scribed modelling clays are more porous than the plastikard and will require a slightly different approach again – I confess to having little experience of either, so returning to my favoured plastikard, the accompanying photograph illustrates the stages from left to right, starting with the bare (in this example) grey material. Pre-coloured red plastikard would still require the same routines. Mix up enamel paint to represent a simple mortar colour such as creamy white and paint this over the entire area. When touch dry, take a thinners-

moistened cloth and wipe across the surface of the plastikard until the faces of the bricks are grey again, leaving the 'mortar' trapped in the courses of the embossed brickwork. If you wish your bricks to appear lighter in some patches, you could leave a few of the brick faces coated in the mortar mix to act as a lighter undercoat which will show through the subsequent coats to create a slight variation in shading which should add character to the brickwork.

Now mix up some brick colour – in this instance Matt Orange (82), Flesh (61), plus Brick Red (70), and, using a 'flattie' brush, gently drybrush across the raised surfaces of the bricks, all the while varying the proportions of the component colours until the bricks take on the correct appearance. The paint build-up also adds extra relief and increases the embossed effect. When touch dry, add a little Tarmac (112) to your mix and gently drybrush, almost at random, over some of the brickwork, blending in a little Matt Black (33) if the Tarmac isn't dark enough, and then, to lighten your brick colour, bung in some Grey (64) and repeat the process. Don't worry if you've been a little heavy-handed and the brick colour has filled up some of the mortar courses, because the optional next stage will overcome that problem.

It's vital that the brickwork is dry before you attempt the next part (ideally wait until the next day), then take your now dry

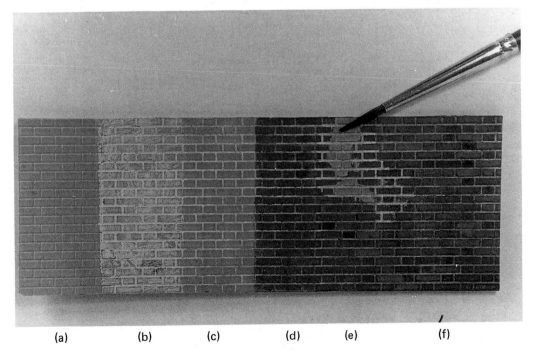

(a) Plain embossed Plastikard. (b) Mortar coloured paint liberally applied. (c) Surface wiped clean, leaving mortar courses filled. (d) Bricks drybrushed with suitable colours. (e) Extra diluted mortar colour applied by capillary action. (f) Yet further drybrushing plus some individual bricks painted.

(a)   (b)   (c)   (d)   (e)   (f)

My version of a small warehouse, the original of which backs onto the river in the centre of Lewes, Sussex. The faded lettering reads: 'JAMES FRANKS' — not the owner of the building, just my way of thanking a good friend and highly esteemed resident of Lewes who took several superb photographs of the prototype for me at very short notice.

brickwork and lean it at an angle of about 45 degrees. Make up a very runny mix of enamel thinners and the creamy white mortar colour. I can't offer you exact proportions — you will need to experiment a little until you get it right. I usually put about a teaspoonful of thinners into the lid of the can and drop a couple of blobs of the mortar colour into it and stir well. It should still be pretty runny, but, if too thick, just add more thinners. Having loaded a pointed brush (No. 1 or 2 should be ideal) with the diluted mortar mix, just touch the tip of the brush to the top edge of your brick wall and you will be amazed to see the mortars/thinners run by capillary action down all of the recessed courses so that suddenly all of the bricks will be surrounded by freshly made mortar again. Wait until it has stopped running, then add further brush loads at that point and repeat the procedure until the process has literally run its course.

Adding a little Gunmetal or Matt Black into the very wet courses in odd places

A closer view of the model reveals stained and ravaged brickwork, a distinctive, uneven join between the two buildings, and the differing shades of bricks used in their construction.

will provide variations in the colour of the mortar, giving the wall extra authenticity, plus a little dull matt green blended in on the odd patch to simulate damp mossy growth – say around the base of the wall.

If you don't wait until the original brick paintwork is dry and attempt any of this too soon, the 'mortar' mix will not run freely down the courses and also some of the brick paint will come adrift, leaving a rare old mess.

Once this has dried, you will inevitably find the watery mix has stained the surface of some of the bricks. Check your photos first, because many bricks have just such an appearance, but if you're not content with this effect, just drybrush the surface of the offending items with your selected brick colour until the stains disappear and you reach the desired result. Leave it to dry and then, where appropriate, paint individual bricks in varying shades of the main colour with a tiny pointed brush. It's not necessary to paint the entire face of every brick

Diamond patterned brickwork of model destined for a future project.

because the outer edges of the brick face will retain the previously applied colours and produce an interesting halo effect. You will probably develop cramp in your pinkies after just a short session which will stop you from overdoing this stage. As a final treatment, gently dust the wall with some talcum powder to soften the appearance if you feel there's too much contrast in the colours.

Occasionally, buildings are embellished with some fancy patterns using darker coloured bricks and you can mimic this by painting certain areas to match – an example of which is the photograph of the shop. This all adds interest and breaks up what could be a large expanse of mundane brickwork. On retaining walls and particularly bridge support walls, there are extremes of vertical staining caused by moisture escaping from the earthworks

Above left: Bridge brickwork photographed to show how moisture emerges from behind the retaining wall through the brick courses and then forms vertical stains. Above right: The modelled version produced by drybrushing and smearing the paint in downward motions with a finger. The concrete bearing beam at the top is similarly treated.

Hursley's skew arch bridge shows stained brickwork and mortar courses. The speed restriction sign is lightly drybrushed on its edges just sufficient to simulate encroaching rust.

An assortment of building materials, combining brickwork with flint/rubble mix, plus faded and peeling timber, all topped with an asbestos roof.

Slates on the model are treated as described in the text.

Old slates plus some replacements on the roof of my Plymouth model shop. See how thin these slates really are and how the older ones are covered in lichen growth.

behind, which leach out through the courses and dribble downwards from their various exit points. Find a really damp example and you will see a multitude of colours which will provide you with hours of entertainment in the duplicating thereof!

STONEWORK

This is rather brief because, as with any embossed surface areas, the routines described for brickwork are adapted to suit by simple substitution of the appropriate colours, assuming plastikard is being employed. Again, there is tremendous variation in stone colour and texture dependent upon its origins, and colour photographs are vital to ensure accurate replication. Some examples have a very matt, dull finish such as sandstone – whereas granite looks far more sturdy and has a pronounced sheen when cut. Similarly, flint has an outer sandy colour going to off-white and finally to a metallic grey plus assorted beige speckles. I've simulated this in the single-storey shed which I found at Ventnor on the Isle of Wight. Painting all those individual flint stones left me wondering why I took up this hobby in the first place.

ROOFING

Many layouts are set at such a height that the viewer is naturally looking down upon the roofs of the houses, etc, so it is therefore rather important for these areas to appear natural and not detract from the remainder of the exhibit. Again, applying slates or tiles to a roof can be fairly tiresome and the temptation is to rush through it just to get it over and done with. Whichever method you opt to choose, take your time because the best paint job in the world cannot hide poor workmanship when it can so readily be scrutinised.

Most of my structures have been slate-roofed and I try to paint the slates in one all-over colour, adding just minor variations in shade while the paint is wet. Tarmac (112) is pretty close to the blue-grey slate evident in most of the photographs appropriate for my region, but you will need to do some homework to establish which shades are favoured in your own area.

Once the basic colour has dried, mix up a lighter version of your base colour and gently drybrush the roof in a vertical action – following the laws of gravity. This will highlight the edges of the slates or tiles and bring them into more prominent relief. Don't overdo this part because study of a typical slated roof will show how very thin

some slates are and heavy-handed dry-brushing will make them appear too thick simply by drawing attention to the edges. This can be a problem particularly if you've had to use materials which are a little too thick in the first place and you really need to disguise the edges rather than highlight them. In that case, place more emphasis on the main body of the slate instead.

Slate can vary regionally and some buildings show quite a variety of colours on one roof. Rather than paint each slate a totally different shade, which somehow never looks convincing, try adding in small patches of slightly varied colour while the initial paint application is still wet. You should obtain much softer contrasts by this method which hopefully will do the trick.

Now let this dry completely and, dependent upon how badly your chosen roof has worn, you may wish to take things a stage further by mixing up some well diluted grey/green sludge and liberally applying this by brush all over your roof in top to bottom strokes. (I would suggest a similar consistency to the diluted mortar mix you used on your brickwork in order for it to run freely.) Again, with the mix being very fluid, it should run down all the seams

between each slate by capillary action. A word of caution here, because if your roofing slates are plastikard, the multiple applications of thinners may cause some of them to lift here and there and soften at the same time. This can result in some peculiar wrinkled looking slates which aren't quite authentic! If this does happen, you may need to remove one or two offending items with a scalpel and replace with freshly cut inserts. Paint these in a natural slate colour and in the process you will have created the genuine impression of recently replaced slates. I'm all for making the best of a disaster and frequently have discovered new weathering effects by just such examples of misfortune.

If you've overdone the sludge, just take a cotton bud dipped in thinners and wipe the roof in a top to bottom action to remove the offending grime. This will, at the same time add extra delicate streaks to the roof. A final light dusting with talc will tone things down nicely.

In many instances, birds perch upon the ridges and leave their marks as proof, so you may like to add in some extra off-white streaks in one or two areas. Unless you know for a fact they hold regular meetings

there, don't get too carried away with the blemishes or it may look a little too obvious. Be subtle.

According to the location and direction of the building, it may attract certain types of lichen in patches on some of the slates, and I've found that mixing Matt Yellow (24) with a little Orange (62) and stippling this in very tiny patches, with the addition of plenty of talc, can create the illusion of a particular type of lichen growth. When dry, this can be gently drybrushed with a lighter version of the yellow/orange mix to add further highlights.

If this is too long-winded for you, an alternative (after the main roof paint has dried) is to paint fresh tiny patches of the roof in your chosen slate colour again and, whilst wet, mix one of the Carr's powders, which is a yellow ochre colour, with a little of the very orangey rust powder, and ladle tiny amounts of the blended powders onto the wet paint. When you're certain the paint has dried underneath, either tip the building upside-down over a piece of paper or gently blow across the surface to remove any surplus pigment. You should be left with a fair representation of natural growth. Please refer to photographs again if unsure

Corrugated iron huts at Hursley.

BARRY NORMAN

how this should look. I know I do witter on a bit about reference to photos, but if you copy precisely what you see and not what you think you might see ... there's that motto again. Mother Nature has already got it right so just copy her.

CORUGATED IRON

A favourite of mine, I really enjoy using it where possible because it is so utilitarian and always adds a natural rustic and run-down air to any set piece. Even freshly painted, it still looks cheap and cheerful and that appeals somehow. Once more, I use Slater's Plastikard which, although not quite so deeply corrugated as some metal alternatives, is very simple to use. The weathering procedures are fairly straight-forward, according to how much decrepi-tude the real thing has acquired.

For relatively sound, painted finishes, paint the entire surface with its top coat and leave to dry. Now mix up a lighter shade of this colour and drybrush the ridges of the corrugations. This will highlight them and at the same time, really emphasise the furrows. When dry, the latter may be further enhanced by running a diluted dull grimy mixture over the surface leaving murky deposits in the gullies. The extent of your weathering can be gauged by the

The goods shed with its corrugations highlighted by gentle drybrushing with a paler shade of its green paint. A mild brush application of diluted grime accentuates the furrows and leaves small staining rings around the securing bolts.

BARRY NORMAN

amount of abuse you are attempting to reproduce. Where the paint has worn away but not actually rusted, drybrush the ridges with a light blue/grey such as Sky Blue (122) plus a little Matt Concrete (95) to suggest the primed metal underneath showing through. If the paint is really well worn, it can be given further maltreatment by drybrushing the ridges again in some rust shades such as Bauxite (133) mixed with Orange (82) or a touch of Leather (62), darkening the colours with Metalcote Gunmetal for older rust. If you're careful here and can leave the outer edges of the ridges still showing some of the 'primer' grey colour, it will appear as though the paint has worn right through from topcoat to rust with all the stages visible.

Once you are happy with the look of things and the paint has completely dried, gently wash the corrugations with a diluted grimy mix to further vary the stains. Hopefully even the black & white photos of the corrugated building will show how much variety and interest can be introduced to the surfaces by these methods.

The areas where the sheets overlap can be emphasised because these parts usually start to corrode from their extremities inwards and this also traps other impurities at the same places. You might try abrading the leading edges of these overlaps with coarse sandpaper until the material becomes thin and crumbly. Added cracks and splits can be introduced with a sharp knife and then these parts can be stippled with talcum powder plus your favourite combination of rust shades. Decrease the stippling as you move away from the fragmented edges, fading out until you reach fairly sound 'metalwork'. This latter part can be duplicated far more easily with an airbrush because you can spray the rust colours and then ease back on the throttle as you move the airbrush away from the edges. It's certainly a lot quicker.

Where the bolts and their washers appear, either run some enamel thinners over these and touch neat gunmetal/bauxite to the heads of the bolts so that dark stains are left when dry, or if you have a fine airbrush you can gently puff tiny patches of dark rust onto these boltheads and their immediate surrounds. As with all of the weathering processes, the airbrush isn't a prerequisite, but can be most useful if available.

Carr's weathering powders can be sparingly applied to these same 'rusty' patches and the textured surface will provide a key so that the powdered pigments can adhere.

I built this large corrugated structure after discovering its prototype on the Isle of Wight. Most of the paintwork was quite recent, but, for my version, I decided that the area normally concealed behind a large sliding door was to have been left untouched by the maintenance men.

This closer view shows the ridges losing their topcoat, revealing primer beneath and other areas rusting away merrily. The temptation was to treat the entire building this way, but this one decrepit area makes for a more interesting model. Understatement rather than the opposite.

Two views of a small weighbridge office based loosely upon that which once lurked in Plymouth Friary yard but alas now demolished. The original had a slate roof, but for my own needs, a corrugated asbestos version was installed.

CORRUGATED ASBESTOS

This material has larger scale corrugations and, in reality, is generally unpainted simply because it doesn't need to be, having few natural corrosive enemies to worry about. It can't rust and will withstand most that the elements hurl at it. Its colour is not unlike concrete or cement (which we'll deal with in a moment) and I would suggest you try mixing Natural Wood (110) with Grey (64) or perhaps more logically, Concrete (95) which is a lighter grey and apply these together with some stippled-in talcum powder where you are representing walling. When dry, staining can be introduced by mixing some watery Tarmac (112) and letting this run down the channelling, some of which will become absorbed into the sludgy talc/paint and look quite realistic. Similarly, you can drybrush the surface with darker and lighter shades of the grey/brown mixes to draw attention to the textured nature of the asbestos.

Particularly noticeable on certain roofs constructed from this material is a build-up of deposits from nearby trees or just natural surface growth of lichens, etc. The talc is probably not coarse enough to simulate this – particularly in 7mm – and I recently experimented with some very fine brown dust like scatter (I think it was the Woodland Scenics Soil) sifted onto the wet paint through a tea strainer. This was appropriate for some parts of the roof but a little too coarse for others and I resorted to using sieved soil dust from the garden. Don't overdo the application here because we're striving for a speckled effect and if you

For this roof, I sieved garden soil dust onto the painted surface whilst still wet. Asbestos roofs seem to attract this moss and lichen growth.

apply too much powder, the corrugations will disappear entirely. When all is dry, the brown dust can either be left in its natural state or highlighted by drybrushing with lighter shades of the brown colouring. More of the yellow/orange lichen may be drybrushed or, in the case of the Carr's powders, stippled onto small patches of the dust, much as we did with the roof slates. The photographs of the single-storey sheds and the weighbridge office should help to clarify the above.

Whilst working with these particular colour groups, we may as well discuss:

CONCRETE

In reality, a fairly mundane and uninspiring material which, even when new, never seems to look anything other than depressing! I really cannot get excited about concrete in the real world, but for modelling buildings, it's very satisfying to portray and I try to incorporate it into at least one building on a layout if at all possible.

After 'distressing' the Plastikard, paint plus sprinkled-on talcum powder does the job for concrete.

Left: *A telegraph pole does not at first glance excite much interest, but peer more intently at one and see the way in which the knots and grain have absorbed the creosote. Lots of variety here, if you take the time to look.* Right: *A Ratio 7mm example weathered as described in the text.*

The procedure is much the same as for the asbestos – stippling the same colours onto a plain or previously roughened or scarred plastikard surface and while the paint is wet, sifting small clouds of talc onto the paintwork through a tea strainer or very finely meshed small sieve. Let some of the talc soak up the paint and stay where it lands in tiny clumps, or, alternatively, blow across the surface of the paint which will scatter the talc more evenly and leave a much finer textured finish. When all is dry, the raised detail can be highlighted by drybrushing with lighter greys and also darker grey/blacks which produces a wetherbeaten effect. Occasionally you will observe the aggregate content of the concrete showing through where some of the cement has worn away and gentle stippling with a coarse brush which has been dipped in an orange/bauxite mix and then wiped almost clean will create an appropriate result – sort of 'dry stippling' rather than brushing.

The yellow/orange lichen seems to love concrete walling and ridges and these small patches will add a dash of colour to its more dull and boring grey/beige appearance. An additional splash of grimy thinners applied when all is completely hardened and dry will add more body and contrast to its appearance. A final dusting with talc should soften things and add a little sparkle to the finish.

WOOD

There's really not a lot to say that hasn't already been covered in the section dealing with open wagons and box vans, because the procedures for doors and window frames, etc, are all related, and it's just a matter of studying your photos to decide which weathering methods are most appropriate. Perhaps just a few observations regarding creosoted planks, sleepers or telegraph poles, which we haven't studied closely before, might be of assistance.

I pondered for some considerable time how best to represent this virtually indescribable greyish, brownish almost at times silvery blend of colours which is how worn creosoted wood appears to me, and somehow my attempts to get the colours right always failed to reach the mark. So it was by accident that the answer presented itself – as is so often the way. I had been working on a wagon whose planks were supposed to be unpainted and rather work-weary, and had adopted my normal routine of blending greys and beiges with a little lighter grey drybrushing, and had left this to dry whilst getting on with the metalwork

The large corrugated iron building's staff entrance! I fastidiously copied as many of the blemishes and other characteristic features of the original as I could which made for quite an absorbing few hours. With a rather plain model, such attention to detail on specific parts of a building is worth the effort.

around it. This metal was also fairly decrepit and I was drybrushing the metalwork with some ordinary Gunmetal (53) and accidentally treated the 'timber' to a swift stroke of the brush. Voila! As it dried, there was that elusively silvery lustre for which I had so long been searching. (Fighting back the tears of joy as the violins swell to a crescendo …) Further delicate streaks applied with a really tiny pointed sable brush and in the direction of the grain, plus the odd dot here and there to suggest knots in the wood, which are usually slightly darker, and there you have it. And why not? – in the words of the other Barry Norman.

For fresher creosoted woodwork, I usually apply Matt Black (33) with a touch of Chestnut Brown (186) all over the area to be treated and when dry, drybrush with the Gunmetal again. The end result is quite pleasing.

ROOFING FELT & TARMAC

These are related to one another, having a bitumastic base and, although differing in texture due to the aggregate content size requirement, the principles are identical. Weathered roofing felt may be simulated by brush painting the Plastikard roof with Tarmac (112) and, while wet, sieving talcum powder onto the surface in fairly even coatings, then blowing across the surface to distribute the talc more evenly. This should be allowed to dry completely, after which talc brushed onto the surface in top to bottom strokes will create delicate streaks. Seams are effected by scribing and

Study of a shed door although it could have been the interior of a wagon if not told otherwise, The method of creating such effects is described in the Wagons chapter.

then filling the ensuing grooves with Tippex typewriter correction fluid. These, once dry, are painted in a darker grey/black colour such as Metalcote Gunmetal, then lightly polished to represent neat bitumen. The Tippex is also used to represent creases in the material in the same way as for the box van roofs we described earlier. These ripples (which should be applied before

painting), can be drybrushed in a lighter shade to highlight them. Again, cracked and flaking felt may be a requirement and the Maskol routine which we used for the damaged van roof would be appropriate here.

For Tarmac, the same initial routine applies but slightly more talc should be sprinkled onto the wet paint surface because it is usually a little coarser than roofing felt – although not always as it depends upon the quality of the road surface or perhaps station platform and its state of repair. Damaged sections which have been subsequently attended to may be represented by further applications of Tarmac/Gunmetal in small patches plus more liberal sprinklings of talc. When all is dry, vehicle oil stains, skid marks, ruts, etc, will all add extra signs of stress to the surface.

METALWORK

Lastly, I'll touch on general metalwork because it occurs throughout our layouts in some form or another, whether it be a rusty door hinge or a massive steel girder, and really the methods for weathering any of these items are simply adaptations of the routines we used for the 16 ton mineral wagon earlier.

It is rare to see new metalwork which hasn't been given some kind of protective coating once incorporated into a structure – much as we apply primers and topcoats when building kits and for the same reasons, but prior to its installation, it can occasionally be observed in its natural state

Hursley station platform with its smooth tarmac surface utilising talcum powder sprinkled onto the wet paint.

BARRY NORMAN

A further view shows the country lane surface in the background which is equally smooth.

BARRY NORMAN

The approach to Hursley, with well-kept permanent way, whilst, in contrast, the less frequently used track is overgrown and bearing a darker shade of rust.
BARRY NORMAN

when left in a heap in a goods yard or when transported as wagon loads. Even then it is likely to issue forth from the foundry with an oily coating as a simple temporary measure, but, often as not, this will be insufficient to prevent the ravages of nature having a bash at it. Usually the ends of rails or girders are the first to be attacked, being more porous at these vulnerable points, and often a quite garish bright orange rust will quickly form. Try Orange (82) with a little Leather (62) stippled onto these ends which make quite a marked contrast from the natural steel colouring of the main slab sides. The exposed edges of the girders will also start to tarnish swiftly. As for the smoother sides, we have to decide precisely what colour steel really is, and here it's rather down to checking photographs again. There are many pots of paint labelled 'Steel' or 'Aluminium' but I don't believe any of these quite get it right. I prefer to use the Metalcote Gunmetal or Polished Steel as a basis, with variations of these colours blended in whilst wet, and, when all is dry, gently polishing the paintwork with a finger or cotton bud to bring out an authentic sheen. If the metalwork has been sitting on its wagon parked in a siding for some time, then rust will probably have taken quite a strong hold on things by now and you're into the realms of stippling plus talc followed by weathering powders until the steelwork looks fairly scruffy.

Rails, once installed on their sleepers, become tarnished almost immediately, and for main running lines I spray the entire rail with a blend of Orange (82), Leather (62) and Matt Black (33), adjusting the colours as I go along to provide variation, with additional puffs of Metalcote Gunmetal/ Grey (64) where I wish to show gatherings of oily sludge, such as around fishplates or where a loco has been standing. Naturally you can use a paint brush if you wish but be careful not to obscure all of the detail by applying paint too thickly.

The top surface of the rail should ideally be cleaned whilst the paint is still fresh, but, if everything has dried, use a cotton bud wetted with thinners (enamel or cellulose according to how long you have allowed the paint to harden). If you have nickel silver rail, you may wish to make this appear less yellow by rubbing the good old Birch-wood Casey Liquid Gun Blue onto the top surfaces with a cotton bud until the nickel silver changes colour to a more blue/grey steel colour. Clean the surface with water to neutralise the chemical and finally polish the rail head with a cloth or polishing mop

in your modelling electric drill. Of course, if you're using steel rail in the first place, the Gun Blue could be useful if you would like to actually chemically rust your rails. I would suggest you experiment on a spare piece of rail with the chemical first until you're certain how it will react.

For sidings where the rail has really been left to the elements, the above procedures apply, but I would recommend stippling in some talc plus the addition of Bauxite (133)

Even the most apparently insignificant items require weathering if they are to appear realistic. These Peco 4mm scale skips are simply stippled and drybrushed using a suitable metallic rust mix to simulate the results of everyday clouts and scrapes.

and added Gunmetal (53) since these tracks are usually a lot darker than the main running lines. Rails which see regular traffic become coated in brake dust, which is where the Leather (62) comes in, whereas the little used lines don't receive this coating. If the rails aren't used by stock at all, then as well as the webs, the rail heads can also be left painted. Don't forget the rail chairs which should be similarly treated, and, if airbrushing, don't worry if some

This could almost be a photograph of part of a mineral wagon, steel door or any other object which is prone to rust. Similar corrosion can be found on steelwork of many types and your models will benefit visually by reproducing these effects accordingly. This particular process is described in the section dealing with the 16-ton mineral wagon.

114

The Art of Weathering

BARRY NORMAN

paint oversprays onto the sleepers or the ballast – look at the real thing and you will see the stains immediately under the rails and around the chairs where the rust has leached from the metalwork into the timber.

As with all of these materials, study the prototype and if you can fastidiously copy that, it should all appear authentic.

From this last chapter, you will hopefully have gathered how readily the procedures we have described along the way can be adapted to just about any material you choose to simulate.

CONCLUSION

I have to draw a halt somewhere and to witter on any longer would probably become tedious in the extreme. One must know when to leave the stage which is ideally before the audience starts to fidget, doze off or throw things! I suspect this may be that moment.

As we've pottered along, I've attempted to guide you through a multitude of procedures – some fairly complex and others relatively simple – and the possible variations on any or all of these processes are almost endless. You may find it all a little bewildering at first and in some instances will undoubtedly decide to use a few of your own ideas instead of those I've described – marvellous, that's exactly as it should be. As I intimated at the beginning,

the methods I use aren't the 'be all and end all' of weathering, they're simply set routines which I have found suit me. If you can think of alternative procedures which prove better for you and which bring about the results you seek, then use them.

I have described in as much detail as I can how to apply the various techniques discussed and you will hopefully find these guidelines useful, but as with any new venture, only your own patience and steadily acquired skill will enable you to become accomplished in the art.

As I have repeated from time to time, 'restraint' is often the key word. Overdone, weathering can look far too contrived and can easily defeat the purpose of the whole exercise – namely to make your models

look more realistic. Be subtle and don't become too distressed if it doesn't always work out as you want – just persevere. I've been at it a long time and I still make a complete hash of it every now and then. I should be pleased if the methods discussed have removed some of the mystery, encouraging you to look at this weird and wonderful hobby of ours from a slightly different and I hope more enlightened viewpoint. At the very least it should set you thinking.

Remember – the best compliment you can receive from a casual observer is not how well you've weathered a model, rather the ultimate accolade:

"Doesn't it look real!"

MOST COMMONLY USED WEATHERING PAINT COLOURS

J.P. (Perkins) or Humbrol

Black	(No. 33)	Leather	(No. 62)
Orange	(No. 82)	Gunmetal	(No. 53)
Grey	(No. 64)	Concrete	(No. 95)
Natural Wood	(No. 110)	Tarmac	(No. 112)
Satin Bauxite	(No. 133)	Gloss Tan	(No. 9)

Humbrol

'Metalcote'   Gunmetal
'Metalcote'   Polished Steel

Acrylic (J.P. or Humbrol)

Matt Varnish
Satin Varnish
Gloss Varnish

COLOUR SUPPLEMENT

With her oily rods, light dusting and highlighted details achieved by polishing and drybrushing, she looks a powerful beast. Buffers, couplings and copperwork were all chemically tarnished using Liquid Gun Blue. Neutralising the chemical with water stopped the copperwork going too dark.

Engineering at its best — a 7mm scale '61XX' scratchbuilt by Tony Reynalds and just begging to be lightly weathered.

Hopefully looking just a little more authentic after I had a bash at it.

She's still quite clean, but the delicate spraying and removing again has left tiny stains around each rivet, with a further partial spray to indicate fresh activity. Each wheel spoke is drybrushed and polished to bring the detail to life. It's a pleasure to work with such an inspirational model — no disguising of errors in construction such as are found on my own creations. Wonderful!

Although a small loco, the 'B4' was one of the most powerful 0—4—0s. She is fairly grimy, with signs of her identity marks having been cleaned on an earlier occasion but now fresh coatings of grime are building up again.

This view shows the soot and ash scuffed and polished by the crew's feet. Simply sprayed, this area would not have shown all the detail, but drybrushed and polished, colour and texture catch the eye.

Although well covered with various shades of grime, her identifying insignia are still easily visible. Gentle drybrushing highlights all of the rivets and other raised detail.

The chunky power of the 'Black Five' seems evident in this view. The browner shades of weathering on the smoother boiler contrast with the almost gritty feel of the smokebox.

'U' Class 2–6–0 No. 31794 easing forward to take water. Despite being pretty filthy, some of the lining can still be seen and sunlight is reflected from her boiler. A completely matt finish would not look so convincing.
BARRY NORMAN

The emblems and lining really set off the gloss black finish rather nicely. Rails are coated with brake dust and rust, but the fishplates are well oiled.
BARRY NORMAN

Removal of the auto-coupling and addition of extra detail vastly improves this commercial offering from Lima. The colours of the streaks and stains relieve the monotone grey slab sides, and the small paint chips revealing primer beneath add to the effect.

This Lima '31' was weathered using a withdrawn prototype as my guide. It was looking really shoddy and that was how my customer required it to appear. Dirty, faded and chipped paint — what a heap!

Hornby ECC wagon after extensive drybrushed abuse over an off-white coating from the airbrush.

Lima Sea Cow with interior and chute airbrushed and drybrushed.

Polished buffer heads, red lined frames and buffer beams, worn and faded green paint — all transform an otherwise mundane prototype into one of my favourite models.

Geoff Grayson's BR Mk I from the RJH kit comes to life in colour. Brake dust is working its way up the end whilst grime is trapped in the door seams and around the hinges.

Maunsell push/pull set with shining paintwork offset nicely by the polished wood partitions inside. The roofs are grubby as is the end of the open third.
BARRY NORMAN

The last train of the day departing from Hursley with a Peco permanent way open and ABS unfitted brake van.

A Slater's 7mm brake van with rather ramshackle paintwork.

A Slater's 7mm tank wagon posed on its overgrown siding.

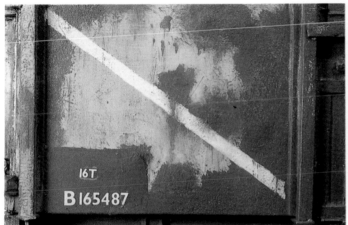

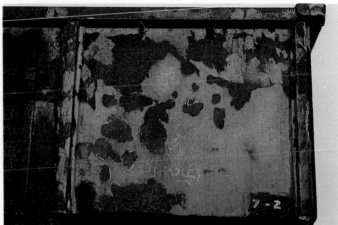

Left: *I enjoy working on mineral wagons because they survived in use in appalling condition throughout the land. No pair ever seem remotely similar, somehow, and that offers so many possibilities for the modeller. Drybrushing and stippling were employed for this one.* Right: *The light has reflected the textures on this wagon quite well. The sparkle of the rusted patches is probably from the Gunmetal (53) paint which contains metallic particles. Talcum powder also has similar visual effects.*

The 7mm ABS fitted open with two replacement planks, left unpainted and treated as per the interior 'woodwork'. Chalk scribblings from pen and Indian ink.

A view over the hedge at Hursley. The siting of the telephone kiosk and mail van was intended to contrast the bright colours with the more restrained greens and beiges of their surroundings.
BARRY NORMAN

Two grimy leviathons frame Hursley's neat signal box.

BARRY NORMAN